Advance Praise for *Hello! Flex 4*

"Everything I know about Flex I learned from Peter. Absolutely true statement. And here's the cool part: I can't think of a better way to learn it...you may not be lucky enough to sit beside him as you learn Flex, but this book is the next best thing. It is Peter's voice you're hearing as you read through the book: hyper-caffeinated, fast-talking, smart, and (extremely!) knowledgeable and opinionated about what makes good Flex code."

Scott Patten, Cofounder
Ruboss Technology Corp.

"I wish I'd had this book when I started developing in Flex. Manages to cover nicely some in-depth topics while still remaining a great introductory text."

Joe Hoover, Web Developer
Tech Lead at RMG Connect

"If you were using time as an excuse, that excuse is now gone...you'll be making cool apps in no time...The fastest read on Flex I've seen to date."

Tariq Ahmed, Author of
Flex 4 in Action

"This book provides an outstanding overview of the latest version of Flex. You'll learn how to build Flex projects for the real world from start to finish."

Sean Moore, Lead Flex Developer
Kannopy, Inc.

Hello! Flex 4

Peter Armstrong

MANNING

Greenwich
(74° w. long.)

For online information and ordering of this and other Manning books, please visit
www.manning.com. The publisher offers discounts on this book when ordered in
quantity. For more information, please contact:

    Special Sales Department
    Manning Publications Co.
    Sound View Court 3B
    Greenwich, CT 06830
    Email: manning@manning.com

 Manning Publications Co.   Development Editor: Cynthia Kane
    209 Bruce Park Avenue   Copyeditor: Liz Welch
    Greenwich, CT 06830   Typesetter: Marija Tudor
                                Cover designer: Leslie Haimes

ISBN: 978-1-933988-76-4

Printed in the United States of America
1 2 3 4 5 6 7 8 9 10 – MAL – 14 13 12 11 10 09

For Caroline and Evan

Brief contents

Contents

Preface

All books have a low point during writing, and this book had a lower one than most. Specifically, this book was born out of *three* almost simultaneous failures at the end of 2008:

- The failure of the Ruboss Framework as a commercial product
- The failure of *Enterprise Flexible Rails* as a book
- The failure of the format of *Hello! Flex 3*

In the immortal words of hip-hop superstar Friedrich Nietzsche,[1] "That which does not kill us makes us stronger," and this perfect storm of failure that ended 2008 for me definitely made me stronger—and made *Hello! Flex 4* a *much* better book.

That is the short version; if you want the long one, read on…

Shortly after *Flexible Rails* was published by Manning in early 2008, I began working full-time on my company Ruboss and recruited a co-founder, Dima Berastau. We were bootstrapping a product called the Ruboss Framework by doing consulting. The Ruboss Framework was licensed under GPL v3 and a commercial license, so it was free for Flex and $499 for the AIR version. I wanted to market the Ruboss Framework by writing a book about it, so I discussed with Mike Stephens at Manning a sequel to *Flexible Rails*, titled *Enterprise Flexible Rails*, which would pick up where *Flexible Rails* left off and lead readers to using the Ruboss Framework for their Flex projects.

---

[1] What, you thought I was quoting German philosopher Kanye West?

In parallel to my working on the Ruboss Framework and *Enterprise Flexible Rails*, Mike approached me in early 2008 and asked if I had any recommendations for someone to write *Hello! Flex 3* for Manning. The publisher was creating a new series of books called "Hello! X," and the format was going to be a fun, lighthearted introduction to a topic, featuring cartoons. In a true Dick Cheney moment, I said, "I pick me." I knew J.D. Frazer (a.k.a. "Illiad," the creator of the web comic *User Friendly*), so I proposed to Manning that they use *User Friendly* cartoons in the *Hello!* series and I made the introduction. Since I had just finished a book about using Flex 3 with Rails, I thought it would be fairly simple to write another one, adding cartoons and removing Rails. Just like runners at the end of a marathon, I must have been on an endorphin rush, since *Hello! Flex 3* seemed easy in comparison to *Flexible Rails*. Mike said that they strongly discourage anyone from trying to write two books at once. However, in a moment of supreme hubris, and against Mike's better judgment, I prevailed. So, I started writing *Hello! Flex 3*.

Over the course of 2008, I wrote six chapters of *Hello! Flex 3*, using the same iterative code example format that I had used in *Flexible Rails*, but with the addition of cartoons. I also wrote two chapters of *Enterprise Flexible Rails*. That sounds respectable, but basically it was a washout. (Hubris breeds nemesis, after all!)

First, *Enterprise Flexible Rails* was selling moderately well for a niche book, but with the direction it was headed, it didn't have a broad enough appeal. Also, the book was not progressing fast enough. It turned out that I didn't have the time, so Mike was right: I shouldn't have attempted two books at once. Mike and I agreed to cancel *Enterprise Flexible Rails*. (Also, Ruboss subsequently changed the name of the Ruboss Framework to the RestfulX framework, made the product free, and changed the license to the MIT license.)

Second, *Hello! Flex 3* had an identity crisis. We realized that "*Flexible Rails* plus cartoons" did *not* make a good *Hello!* series book. *Hello! Flex 3* was going to need to be completely rewritten—both to update the format to one better suiting the series, and also to rewrite the book to target Flex 4 (which was due to be released in the second half of 2009).

So, *Hello! Flex 3* was scrapped, and the code in its six chapters was used as the basis of one chapter in this book: the "SocialStalkr" example in chapter 7, which I rewrote to use Flex 4 and the Spark components. I also realized that the best format for the remainder of the book was that of a fake workshop. I thought it would be funny to do a cartoon mashup, so I drew a stick figure (yes, inspired by that famous web comic) to represent me giving a workshop to the *User Friendly* cartoon characters. This would be a meeting of Web 2.0 (the stick figure) and Web 1.0 (the *User Friendly* characters), with lots of opportunity for humor as well as instruction.

I spent the next three months working ridiculous hours, writing chapters 1–6 from scratch. I got the book done in late summer 2009, and we proceeded to edit and produce the book. Manning excels at the production process, which is one reason their books have such a great reputation.

The story ended happily—and I feel that a really good book is the result.

Acknowledgments

First and foremost, I'd like to thank my wife Caroline for her amazing patience and support throughout the writing of this book—since I was also starting my company Ruboss and attempting to write *Enterprise Flexible Rails* all at the same time. Anyone who has written a book or started a company knows how much time these things take, so the fact that over the past two years I wrote this book, started a company, and attempted to write a second book means that Caroline has made a *lot* of sacrifices.

Second, I'd like to thank my son Evan for his understanding. I managed to have enough time to play "Super Mario Galaxy" and other games with him, but not enough time to finish building the second Lego Mindstorm robot we've been working on. Now I will, and Robogator won't just be a snapping mouth with eyes, but it will have legs and a tail! (Someday I look forward to teaching him how to program these things too...)

I'd also like to thank Dima Berastau. He made huge contributions to Ruboss during 2008, and even contributed a couple of pages to this book and helped with the Yahoo! Maps integration code in chapter 7. The RestfulX Framework is pleasant to work with, and that's Dima's doing. Finally, I made a lot of mistakes during our year of working together building Ruboss 1.0, and I'd like Dima to know that I appreciated the opportunity to work with him.

Next, I'd like to thank Scott Patten. Scott became employee No. 1 at Ruboss in March 2008, and his tireless efforts, coding prowess, and ability to understand the needs of clients has been instrumental to our success. When Dima left and Ruboss pivoted from being Ruboss 1.0 (a company trying to sell a framework) to Ruboss 2.0 (a company building a Web 2.0 product), Scott stepped up and became a true cofounder.

I'd also like to thank Steve Byrne. Not only did Steve jump in at the last minute to do the technical proofreading for me, but he also did a phenomenally thorough job of it. I expected this, since I learned Flex from him (and Matt Wyman) five years ago, so I already knew what depth of knowledge Steve had. Steve knows Flex better than I do, and he's an outstanding architect and technical mind. If Steve ever writes a book, I'll be the first to buy it, and you should be the second.

Next, I'd like to thank Jason McLaren and Ken Pratt, since both of their efforts enabled me to have a lot more time for this book. Also, helping Jason learn Flex sharpened my focus and helped this book; sometimes one forgets what the right questions are.

I'd also like to thank Duane Nickull, Adobe's evangelist in Vancouver, who has been a source of encouragement for me over the years, letting me speak about *Flexible Rails* and RestfulX at his events and letting me chip in a couple paragraphs to his *Web 2.0 Architectures* book.

Next I'd like to thank Dane Brown, who kept me well caffeinated over the year that Ruboss was working out of WorkSpace. Without your espresso macchiatos keeping me going, this book might not have happened at all!

I'd also like to thank J.D. and David from *User Friendly* for letting Manning use the *User Friendly* cartoons in the *Hello!* series. J.D., I've had a good time putting words in the mouths of your characters, and I hope you get a couple laughs out of them if you read this book.

Special thanks to the following reviewers who read the manuscript at different stages during its development, taking time out of their busy schedules to provide feedback—their comments made this a better book: Andrew Siemer, Doug Warren, Joe Hoover, Justin Tyler Wiley, Robert Dempsey, Sean Moore, Tariq Ahmed, Tony Obermeit, Philipp K. Janert, Jeffery Pickett, Robert Glover, Reza Rahman, Maris Whetstone, Edmond Begoli, Dusty Jewett, Andrew Rubalcaba, Nikolaos Kaintantzis, Jeff Pickett, and Lester Lobo.

Finally, I'd like to thank the team at Manning.

First, I'd like to thank Marjan Bace and Mike Stephens for having the idea for the *Hello!* series and for letting me contribute to it.

Second, I'd like to thank development editor Cynthia Kane. Cynthia endured the brunt of the format frustrations, maintaining her cool and sense of humor while I vented about "this isn't a book, it's a science project!" and other similar sentiments. I appreciate her encouragement and composure, especially as I hit reset on the whole book and started over. I'm not sure if she believed I would actually ever finish the book, but if she didn't, she did a good job of hiding that fact.

Next, I'd like to thank Liz Welch for her amazing job of copyediting. I needed to do a few passes through each chapter, so that I could see her formatting changes and her insertions and deletions without them drowning out her comments. The best compliment I can pay her is that the book still felt like my writing, only better—not some "designed by committee" neutered prose. The second-best compliment I can pay her is that Maureen Spencer's job of proofreading actually seemed pretty easy. Of course, Maureen is great, but this seems like an easier trip than *Flexible Rails* was for her. So Liz and Cynthia get credit for that.

One more thing: I'd like to thank Ruboss's clients. Besides being fun to work with, without you we wouldn't be able to build our own product and I wouldn't have been able to write this book. *(Oh yeah, we wouldn't eat either!)* We love you.

About this book

You can think of this book as a two- or three-day workshop, transcribed into book form—*and much cheaper*! The stick figure character is a stand-in for me teaching the workshop, and the cartoon characters are your classmates. The questions they'll ask or the opinions they express may be your own.

I have two goals for this book: first, to teach Flex 4 in a way that exposes you to real-world Flex problems in an accessible way, and second, to have a bit of fun with this book, without being cutesy, distracting, or insulting. The purpose of the cartoons in this introductory section is to provide an amusing backstory; in the rest of the book I'll use them to draw attention to important concepts.

Who should read this book

You should read this book if you're a software developer who is either completely new to Flex or new to Flex 4 in particular. My assumption is that you do know how to write computer programs, and that you know how to use the web. I don't explain either of those, and if something is better referred to by a URL instead of paraphrased (poorly), that's what I do. If you've done a bit of Flex programming or seen articles or blog posts about Flex, that's great—but I don't assume any Flex knowledge in this book. Also, if (like me) you've already shipped production Flex 1, 2, or 3 code, you can still read this book to learn Flex 4—since the book is short and fast-paced, my hope is that blasting through it will get you up to speed faster than any alternative. Finally, since this book includes 27 self-contained examples, if you already know what's in one of them, you can just skip it and move on to the next one.

How this book is organized

A TWITTER MASHUP APP? DO I LOOK LIKE ASHTON KUCHER?

Briefly, this book is divided into seven chapters. The first six chapters contain 26 workshop sessions, and every example is stand-alone. These examples are toy examples, focused on what you're trying to learn in that workshop session—and nothing else. (Most of the workshop session examples fit on one or two pages, with the exception of the Only Connect game we'll build in workshop session 14.) In the last chapter, we'll build a real Flex 4 application. This chapter is essential, since it provides you with the big picture that toy examples can't provide. Furthermore, it will teach you Cairngorm, which is the dominant Flex 4 application framework.

Oh yeah, the application: it's called SocialStalkr, and it's a Twitter and Yahoo! Maps mashup. (Can you get any more Web 2.0 compliant than that?) Besides, there are actual books entirely about Twitter now, so it's like you're getting a free book here.

About the code

All source code in listings or in text is in a `fixed-width font like this` to separate it from ordinary text. Method and function names, object properties, XML elements, and attributes in text are presented using `this same font`. In many cases, the original source code has been reformatted: we've added line breaks and reworked indentation to accommodate the available page space in the book.

Code annotations accompany many of the listings, highlighting important concepts. Numbered cue balls link to explanations of the code that follow the listings.

The source code for all the code examples in the book is available from the publisher's website at www.manning.com/HelloFlex4.

Author Online

Purchase of *Hello! Flex 4* includes free access to a private web forum run by Manning Publications where you can make comments about the book, ask technical questions, and receive help from the author and from other users. To access the forum and subscribe to it, point your web browser to www.manning.com/HelloFlex4. This page provides information on how to get on the forum once you're registered, what kind of help is available, and the rules of conduct on the forum.

Manning's commitment to our readers is to provide a venue where a meaningful dialogue between individual readers and between readers and the author can take place. It's not a commitment to any specific amount of participation on the part of the author, whose contribution to the book's forum remains voluntary (and unpaid). We suggest you try asking the author some challenging questions, lest his interest stray!

The Author Online forum and the archives of previous discussions will be accessible from the publisher's website as long as the book is in print.

About the author

Peter Armstrong is the cofounder of Ruboss Technology Corp., a Vancouver, BC, company focusing on Adobe Flex and Ruby on Rails development and consulting, typically using the RestfulX framework. He's the author of *Flexible Rails* (www.manning.com/armstrong), the book that inspired the creation of the MIT-licensed RestfulX framework for building RESTful Flex applications that easily integrate with server-side frameworks like Ruby on Rails. He was a key part of the team that won the 2006 Adobe MAX Award for RIA/Web Development, and is a frequent conference speaker on using Flex and Rails together.

Peter's blog is http://peterarmstrong.com. You can follow him on Twitter at @peterarmstrong. Peter's email address is peter@ruboss.com.

About *Hello!* books

At Manning, we think it should be just as much fun to learn new tools as it is to use them. And we know that fun learning gets better results. Our *Hello!* series demonstrates how to learn a new technology without getting bogged down in too many details. In each book, *User Friendly* cartoon characters offer commentary and humorous asides, as the book moves quickly from Hello World into practical techniques. Along the way, readers build a unique hands-on application that leverages the skills learned in the book.

Our *Hello!* books offer short, lighthearted introductions to new topics, with the author and cartoon characters acting as your guides.

1

Getting started

In this chapter, you'll learn how to get Flex 4 and how to build a few basic Flex 4 apps. Your goal is to grasp the basic structure and syntax of a Flex 4 application. We'll also explore a high-level picture of the Flex 4 ecosystem.

Why Flex 4?

Chances are you already know why you want to use Flex, so I won't bore you. In case you don't, what follows is the one-paragraph version.

Flex 4 is a sexy framework that lets you write code that feels more like coding a desktop application—except it runs inside the Flash Player. Because it targets the Flash Player, you can build new rich Internet applications (RIAs) without worrying about browser compatibility nonsense, JavaScript, CSS, and so

37SIGNALS IS SELLING
SUBSCRIPTIONS TO
TODO LISTS...

...CHARGING HOW MUCH?

MORE THAN WE CHARGE
OUR CUSTOMERS FOR
INTERNET ACCESS

...AND THAT'S JUST FOR ONE OF THEIR PRODUCTS!

SO LET'S BUILD A WEB 2.0 THINGY

on. Because Flex 4 targets one platform (Flash 10), you don't have to worry about platform compatibility issues. The write once, run anywhere (WORA) dream that client-side Java programmers had—before it turned into write once, debug everywhere—can finally be realized, but with Flex. Flex achieves what previous technologies such as Java applets failed miserably in attempting: applications that feel like desktop applications but that run inside any modern web browser on Windows and Mac. We can use Flex 4 to build RIAs today that look and feel more like Web 3.0 than many of the "me too [point oh]" sites you see copying 37signals and each other today.

Flex 4 overview

Now that you're excited about Flex 4, let's take a deep breath and get an overview of the platform. This section will present a high-level overview; don't worry if you don't understand a particular point here; rest assured I'll explain it later.

In Flex 4, we write code in MXML (XML files with an .mxml extension; M for Macromedia, the company that created Flex and that was acquired in 2005 by Adobe) and ActionScript (text files with an .as extension) files and compile them into an SWF file (that is, a Flash movie), which runs in the Flash Player. This SWF is usually referenced by an HTML file, so that when a user with a modern web browser loads the HTML file, it plays the Flash movie (prompting the user to download Flash 10 if it's not present). The SWF contained in the web page can interact with the web page it's contained in and with the server it was sent from.

Even if you've never created a Flash movie in your life, don't consider yourself a designer, and wouldn't recognize the Timeline if you tripped over it, you can use Flex to create attractive applications that run in the Flash Player. Flex development is easily learned by any intermediate-level developer with either web (HTML and JavaScript) or desktop UI (such as Windows Forms or Java Swing) programming experience. A Flex 4 application is just a Flash movie (SWF), which lives inside a web page loaded by a web browser that has Flash 10 installed.

Flex vs. Ajax? Flex and Ajax?

Now that we have seen what Flex is, let's consider the main alternative to Flex: Ajax. (Silverlight doesn't count—*yet*—since it doesn't have a large enough installed base to be a pragmatic choice for a consumer-facing application.)

The question of when to use Flex, when to use Ajax, and when to use both is extremely controversial. There's no one right answer: it depends on many factors, including the size of your application, the skills of your developers, how important search engine optimization is, and so on. Furthermore, as both Flex and Ajax frameworks evolve, the answer itself evolves. That said, there's one question I like to use: "Are you building a publication or an application?" The more "application like" what you're building is, the better a fit Flex usually is. (Another way of thinking about this is to ask yourself if you could visualize your app being or competing with a desktop application.)

Getting Flex 4 and Flash Builder 4

So, since this is a book about Flex 4, and since you're presumably interested enough in Flex 4 to be reading or browsing it, the next step is for us to actually download Flex 4 and play with it. Somewhat confusingly, Flex 4 applications are built using something called Flash Builder 4. (In Flex 1, 2, and 3 this was called Flex Builder.) The marketing rationale for this is as follows: Flex applications can be built in

FLASH BUILDER?
BUT MY IDE IS
VIM ON LINUX...

conjunction with designers using something called Flash Catalyst, so it makes sense for them to both be called Flash Something, to emphasize that they play nicely together. Second, Flex applications are compiled into Flash movies (SWFs), just as Flash applications developed in Adobe Flash CS4 are compiled into SWFs. However, since the code editor in Flex Builder 3 was so much better than in Flash CS4, many Flash developers were using Flex Builder to build SWFs, without actually using the Flex framework. Or, they'd use Flex Builder and Flash CS4 together. So, Adobe realized that since they had Flash CS4 and Flash Catalyst, they should rename Flex Builder to Flash Builder to fit in.

Looking a little deeper, the real reason Flex Builder could be renamed Flash Builder is that Flex has been so successful in making the Flash Platform

ERWIN, WHAT'S EASIER TO
BUILD GUIS IN THAN AJAX?

OH! I KNOW
THIS ONE!
ALMOST
ANYTHING!!

HOW ABOUT FLASH?

WOW, I DIDN'T KNOW
YOU'D BECOME A DESIGNER!?

something that's considered suitable for enterprise use, not something that's dismissed as intended for games and annoying ads. So, instead of the Flex name having to essentially run away from the Flash brand, it can be used for the open source Flex framework and all the corporate branding can be Flash.

Let's begin by downloading Flash Builder 4. Currently it's available at http://labs.adobe.com/technologies/flashbuilder4/; once the final release of Flex 4 is made, this URL will change and you'll find the new URL on Adobe.com easily enough (hint: Google). A trial version

YOU'RE RIGHT, A.J. IS
THE DESIGNER, NOT ME...

UM...
SILVERLIGHT?

is available that should last long enough for you to follow along with this book. Download the stand-alone version, not the Eclipse plug-in

version, if you want to follow along with the book verbatim.

Flash Builder is Adobe's Eclipse-based IDE for building Flex applications. However, you can also do Flex development using the Flex Software Development Kit (SDK) without Flash Builder: just use your favorite text editor and the command-line compiler that comes with the SDK. This book won't go into how to do that, since most people will end up using Flash Builder.

Should I use Flash Builder Or JUST the Flex SDK?

While the SDK is free, using it isn't as easy as using Flash Builder. So, even if you plan to use the SDK, I recommend using Flash Builder to learn Flex: not only do you get to defer your decision long enough to finish the book (during which time you may decide you like Flash Builder enough to pay for it), you'll also learn Flex faster with Flash Builder providing code-completion support and the design mode, which lets you drag and drop Flex components to lay out a UI.

Beginning the workshop

With this completed, we begin the workshop sessions. These workshop sessions will be grouped into chapters containing thematically related sessions. However, each of these is stand-alone, so they all begin on new pages.

Each workshop session is a separate project in the code zip file. You can follow along with each workshop session by creating a new project in Flash Builder 4. Just choose File > New > Flex Project to open the New

Flex Project dialog. Enter a name for the project in the Project name field and click Finish. It doesn't matter what you name the projects; I named them all session01, session02, and so on in the code zip file. However, note that the project name is used to name the main application, so if you want the main application to be named appropriately, use CamelCase for the name. (In chapter 7, for example, the main application is SocialStalkr so that's what the project should be named.)

SESSION 1   Hello! Flex

This is the first workshop session. In it, we build our first complete Flex application, shown next. Note that the code listing titles show you the exact path to the files in the code zip file, which you can download from http://manning.com/armstrong3/.

session01/src/Hello.mxml

```xml
<?xml version="1.0" encoding="utf-8"?>
<s:Application
  xmlns:fx="http://ns.adobe.com/mxml/2009"
  xmlns:s="library://ns.adobe.com/flex/spark"
  xmlns:mx="library://ns.adobe.com/flex/halo">
  <s:Label="Hello! Flex 4"
    fontSize="128"/>
</s:Application>
```

The root of a Flex application is the `Application` tag. This application contains a

`Label` component with the text "Hello! Flex 4." (For now, ignore the various `xmlns` lines; we'll get to that later in this chapter.) Running this application gives us our first Flex application.

➤➤ Key Points

- Flex applications start with an `Application` tag.
- Flex applications can be built with very little code.

SESSION 2 Dispatching and listening for events

After you get past all the hype about RIAs, Flex development is distinguished by the pervasiveness of two main things: events and data binding. In this session, we'll see how events work; in the next, we'll explore data binding. It may seem odd to dive right into events and data binding before even looking at how Flex

BEHOLD YOUR FIRST FLEX 4 APPLICATION!

applications are structured, but since events and data binding are everywhere in Flex, it's preferable to confront them right away so that the other examples aren't mysterious.

LITERALLY, IN OUR FIRST HOUR OF THE WORKSHOP WE'VE PRODUCED A SEVEN LINE APPLICATION.

MAN, HE'S GOOD. HE'S LOWERING EXPECTATIONS. I WISH I HAD HIS SKILL.

In this section, we'll create an app that contains three `Buttons`: `button1`, `button2`, and `button3`. All `Buttons` dispatch a `MouseEvent` of type `click` (actually `MouseEvent.CLICK`) when the user clicks them; we'll show how to handle this in three different ways in this session. We'll make clicking one of the buttons add the text "Button 1 clicked" (or 2 or 3) to a `Label` text component. For layout, we'll put these `Buttons` and the `Label` into a `VGroup`, as shown here.

session02/src/Hello.mxml

```
<?xml version="1.0" encoding="utf-8"?>
<s:Application
  xmlns:fx="http://ns.adobe.com/mxml/2009"
  xmlns:s="library://ns.adobe.com/flex/spark"
  xmlns:mx="library://ns.adobe.com/flex/halo"
  initialize="init()">
<fx:Script><![CDATA[                                    ← ①
  private function init():void {
    button3.addEventListener(MouseEvent.CLICK, handleClick);    ← ②
  }
  private function handleClick(event:MouseEvent):void {    ← ③
    if (event.target == button2) {
      label.text += 'Button 2 clicked\n';
    } else if (event.target == button3) {
      label.text += 'Button 3 clicked\n';
    }
  }
]]></fx:Script>
  <s:VGroup width="100%">                                 ← ④
    <s:Button id="button1" label="Button 1"
      click="label.text += 'Button 1 clicked\n'"/>         ← ⑤
    <s:Button id="button2" label="Button 2"
      click="handleClick(event)"/>                         ← ⑥
    <s:Button id="button3" label="Button 3"/>
    <s:Label id="label"/>
  </s:VGroup>
</s:Application>
```

① We are including ActionScript 3 code inline for the first time. The `<![CDATA[` and `]]>` is essential inside the `<fx:Script>` tag (so you can type code as you want to without having to worry about special XML character sequences), so Flash Builder adds it for you after you type `<fx:Script>`.

② We call the `init()` function in response to the `initialize` event being automatically dispatched by the application. (Many events, such as initialize, `creationComplete`, and `applicationComplete`, are fired when a Flex application starts; you can write code that handles them. We'll do this later in the book.)

❸ The `handleClick` event handler takes a single `MouseEvent` event parameter; the handler uses the `target` property of the event parameter to determine which button was clicked.

❹ We're putting the Buttons and the `Label` into a `VGroup`, which arranges its children vertically. (Had we used an `HGroup`, they'd have been laid out horizontally.) `VGroup` and `HGroup` are `Group` subclasses.

❺ We can also add a handler for the `click` event in the attribute value.

❻ The `click` event automatically creates a variable called `event`, which in this case is of type `MouseEvent`. We pass this into the handleClick method.

Running the application and clicking the button1, button2, and button3 Buttons in order produces the screenshot shown here.

➡ Key points

- Events can be handled either in the attributes directly or in explicitly written event handler functions.

- Event handlers can be attached to UI components in MXML attribute values or in ActionScript `addEventListener` calls.

- Event objects have a `target` property, which is the source of the event.

- In MXML, components can be nested in `Group` objects. `HGroup` and `VGroup` are subclasses of `Group` that lay out their children horizontally and vertically.

SESSION 3 The Bindable annotation and data binding

Now that we have seen how to use events, let's look at data binding. Data binding is the most unique[1] thing about Flex. It's a powerful feature that's easy to use, and Flex 4 has added a new two-way data binding feature to make it even easier. Data binding is also easy to abuse, with negative consequences for performance (this is covered in great depth in an excellent one-hour presentation titled "Diving in the Flex Data Binding Waters,"[2] by Michael Labriola. Once you're comfortable enough with Flex 4 and data binding that you're curious about how it works under the covers, I highly recommend spending the time to watch this presentation.)

In this session, we'll learn the basics of one-way and two-way data binding. We'll start by building an example that uses one-way data binding twice, to copy the text of two text inputs into each other. We'll also create a Label that uses data binding to show the length of the String in the textInput1.

session03/src/OneWay.mxml

```xml
<?xml version="1.0" encoding="utf-8"?>
<s:Application xmlns:fx="http://ns.adobe.com/mxml/2009"
  xmlns:s="library://ns.adobe.com/flex/spark"
  xmlns:mx="library://ns.adobe.com/flex/halo">
  <s:layout>
    <s:VerticalLayout paddingLeft="5" paddingTop="5"/>
  </s:layout>
  <s:TextInput id="textInput1" text="{textInput2.text}"/>        ⟵——— ❶
  <s:TextInput id="textInput2" text="{textInput1.text}"/>
  <s:Label text="# chars: {textInput1.text.length}"/>
</s:Application>
```

---

[1] Flex data binding is no longer as unique—other frameworks such as JavaFX have added their own implementations of data binding, largely in response to the popularity of data binding in Flex.

[2] http://www.slideshare.net/michael.labriola/diving-in-the-flex-data-binding-waters-presentation?src=embed

1 Each `TextInput`'s text property is bound (with the {} syntax) to the other `TextInput`'s text property.

Running the application, we can type text in and see the following screen.

Well, that was pretty cool! However, let's not stop there: let's get even lazier. What if we want to bind the text properties of both `TextInputs` to each other, but we want to type even less? Flex 4 introduces a new feature to Flex: two-way data binding. Let's see how that works.

session03/src/TwoWay.mxml

```xml
<?xml version="1.0" encoding="utf-8"?>
<s:Application xmlns:fx="http://ns.adobe.com/mxml/2009"
  xmlns:s="library://ns.adobe.com/flex/spark"
  xmlns:mx="library://ns.adobe.com/flex/halo">
  <s:layout>
    <s:VerticalLayout paddingLeft="5" paddingTop="5"/>
  </s:layout>
  <s:TextInput id="textInput1" text="@{textInput2.text}"/>     ◁——————●1
  <s:TextInput id="textInput2"/>
  <s:Label text="# chars: {textInput1.text.length}"/>
</s:Application>
```

1 The `textInput1` text property binding has the even more magical `@{}` syntax, which means "bind this both ways." Note that the text property of the `textInput2` has no binding now, whereas before it used to have the binding `text="{textInput1.text}"`.

Running the application, we see the identical output as before.

Binding isn't just for stupid UI tricks, however: it's primarily used to get data in and out of ActionScript 3 model objects. So, let's create a model object now in ActionScript, and then see how binding works with it. In Flex 4 you write code in one of two ways: in MXML (.mxml) files or in ActionScript 3 (.as) files. We'll create our first ActionScript file now and cover ActionScript more thoroughly in chapter 2.

session03/src/model/Task.as

```
package {
  public class Task {
    [Bindable]
    public var name:String;                    ←————1

    public function Task(name:String = "") {
      this.name = name;
    }
  }
}
```

1 The `Bindable` annotation on the `name` variable ensures it can be the source of a data binding.

Next, let's create a new application that uses this model. (You can copy and paste, then modify the OneWay.mxml application to save time.)

session03/src/BindingToModel.mxml

```
<?xml version="1.0" encoding="utf-8"?>
<s:Application xmlns:fx="http://ns.adobe.com/mxml/2009"
  xmlns:s="library://ns.adobe.com/flex/spark"
  xmlns:mx="library://ns.adobe.com/flex/halo">
<fx:Script>
<![CDATA[
  [Bindable]
  private var _task:Task = new Task("Learn Binding");    ←————1
]]>
</fx:Script>
  <s:layout>
    <s:VerticalLayout paddingLeft="5" paddingTop="5"/>
  </s:layout>
  <s:TextInput id="textInput1" text="{_task.name}"       ←————2
    focusOut="_task.name = textInput1.text;"/>
  <s:TextInput id="textInput2" text="{_task.name}"
    focusOut="_task.name = textInput2.text;"/>
</s:Application>
```

1 We create a new `Task` variable, `_task`, which is `Bindable`, and initialize the `name` property to `Learn Binding`.

❷ The _task variable's `name` property (which is also `Bindable`) is bound to the `text` property of both `textInput1` and `textInput2`.

Running the application, we see that the `TextInputs` are both bound to the `name` property. Typing in either of them and then focusing out (by, say, pressing the Tab key) assigns the text to the model's `name` property, which then updates the other `TextInput`'s text.

But we're feeling lazy; why don't we try using two-way data binding?

session03/src/TwoWayBindingClobbersModel.mxml

```xml
<?xml version="1.0" encoding="utf-8"?>
<s:Application xmlns:fx="http://ns.adobe.com/mxml/2009"
  xmlns:s="library://ns.adobe.com/flex/spark"
  xmlns:mx="library://ns.adobe.com/flex/halo">
<fx:Script>
<![CDATA[
  [Bindable]
  private var _task:Task = new Task("Don't do this!");        ⟵——❶
]]>
</fx:Script>
  <s:layout>
    <s:VerticalLayout paddingLeft="5" paddingTop="5"/>
  </s:layout>
  <s:TextInput id="textInput1" text="@{_task.name}"/>          ⟵——❷
  <s:TextInput id="textInput2" text="@{_task.name}"/>
</s:Application>
```

❶ We initialize a new `Task` just like before.

❷ We use two-way data binding with interesting results.

Once we run the application, we see a surprise. (Well, if you looked at the filename, it's not a surprise.)

The _task.name got clobbered by the initially blank text of the TextInputs! (Note that typing in them does work, however.) So, be careful, especially with two-way data binding.

Now that we introduced events and data binding, let's see what a slightly larger Flex application looks like, so that we can explore the structure of Flex applications.

➤➤ Key points

- Data binding "magically" copies the value of one property to another property. (Well, it's not magic: PropertyChangeListeners are used. But for the purposes of chapter 1 of this book, it's magic.)

- For data binding to work (and not generate compiler warnings), the [Bindable] annotation must be used on the property that's the source of the data binding as well as on the variable that contains the reference to the Object with the property in question.

- Two-way data binding saves time when dealing with UI components, but be careful when using it with models.

SESSION 4   Flex application structure overview

Now that we've seen the required Hello World example (this is a Hello book after all!), let's get a sense of the structure of a real Flex application by building one. Specifically, we're going to build a to-do list. We want to build something like this screenshot.

```
 ◯ ◯ ◯                        TodoList.html
 ◄ ► ⟳ ⊠ +   file:///Users/peter/hf4/code/ch( ▾   Q▾ Google

 Todo List
 New Task  tweet how much you like this book and pay my mortgage|          Create
 ┌──────────────────────────────────────────────────────────────────┐
 │ build a todo list                                                  │
 │ finish reading chapter 1                                           │
 │                                                                    │
 │                                                                    │
 │                                                                    │
 │                                                                    │
 └──────────────────────────────────────────────────────────────────┘
                               Delete
```

This application has a panel with a title of "Todo List," a label with the text "New Task," a text input to enter the new task name, a button for the user to click to create the new task, a big area to list tasks, and a typically overstuffed delete button. (We need at least one gratuitously huge button if we're going to be Web 2.0 compliant! There's no benefit to the panel itself, but it looks nicer than just putting the controls directly in the application—it lets us pretend we're putting *some* thought into design.)

Next, we're going to build this UI. We'll lay out the application UI with MXML, and add logic with Action-Script. (XML is a good markup language for laying out a UI, but it's a terrible language to write real procedural logic in. Thankfully, Flex doesn't force us to do that!) We'll see how we can introduce behavior by adding ActionScript 3 code to both our MXML file (in a Script tag) and to a stand-alone ActionScript 3 file.

Note that the purpose of this workshop session is just to show the big picture; the details of how everything works aren't especially important right now. (I'll explain them at a very high level so that the example makes a bit of sense, but I don't want us to get bogged down.) I want this session to give you a sense of the big picture, of why we're here and what we're trying to do. We'll untangle the details in the workshop sessions ahead.

First, we create a new Task ActionScript class, which is inside a text file with an .as extension. In Flex 4 you write code in one of two ways: in MXML (.mxml) files or in ActionScript 3 (.as) files. (You can actually create multiple classes in one file, but we'll ignore that for now.)

We're going to create this Task class inside a package, specifically the com.pomodo.model package. Flex supports packages in the same way that languages such as Java do, and the backward domain name syntax is a convention just as it is in Java. So, next we create a com\pomodo\model directory structure in the src directory. (Pomodo is just a meaningless fake company name, derived from the Italian word "pomodoro"—I like to do book examples using the Pomodo name since I own the pomodo.com domain name and thus can do what I want with it. So, since pomodo.com would be its domain name, the backward domain name for use in package names is com.pomodo.)

session04/src/com/pomodo/model/Task.as

```
package com.pomodo.model {                                    ←——— ❶
    public class Task {
        [Bindable]
        public var name:String;                               ←——— ❷

        public function Task(name:String = "") {              ←——— ❸
            this.name = name;
        }
    }
}
```

❶ This is the com.pomodo.model package. ActionScript 3 typically uses the same "backwards domain name" convention as Java, so we create a com.pomodo.model.Task class in the com\pomodo\model.

2 We're also creating a variable called name of type String, which we're indicating can be the source of a data binding with the [Bindable] annotation. Briefly, this annotation means that other code can be automatically notified when the value changes.

3 We're creating a constructor, with a default value of an empty String for the Task name parameter. Since this parameter has a default value, we can omit it and invoke the constructor with no arguments. In this constructor, we set the name variable to the name passed in, using the this keyword to establish which name we're referring to.

NOTE   ActionScript 3 supports packages with fewer restrictions than it did in ActionScript 2. It also supports namespaces. There are many details about what you can and can't do with classes, packages, and namespaces; we'll keep things simple and use the "one class per file" and "package in its folder" approach because it's the most straightforward.

Next, we lay out the UI and add code to create and destroy Tasks.

session04/src/TodoList.mxml

```
<?xml version="1.0" encoding="utf-8"?>
<s:Application
  xmlns:fx="http://ns.adobe.com/mxml/2009"
  xmlns:s="library://ns.adobe.com/flex/spark"
  xmlns:mx="library://ns.adobe.com/flex/halo">
<fx:Script>                                              ← 1
<![CDATA[
  import mx.collections.ArrayCollection;                 ← 2
  import com.pomodo.model.Task;

  [Bindable]
  private var _tasks:ArrayCollection = new ArrayCollection();  ← 3

  private function createTask():void {                   ← 4
    _tasks.addItem(new Task(newTaskTI.text));
  }

  private function deleteSelectedTask():void {           ← 5
    _tasks.removeItemAt(taskList.selectedIndex);
  }
```

```
]]>
</fx:Script>
  <s:Panel title="Todo List" width="100%" height="100%">        ◁──────── 6
    <s:VGroup width="100%" height="100%">                 ◁────── 7
      <s:HGroup width="100%" verticalAlign="middle">      ◁───── 8
        <s:Label text="New Task"/>                        ◁───── 9
        <s:TextInput id="newTaskTI" width="100%"
          enter="createTask()"/>                          ◁───── 10
        <s:Button label="Create"click="createTask()"/>    ◁───── 11
      </s:HGroup>
      <s:List id="taskList" width="100%" height="100%"
        labelField="name"                                 ◁───── 12
        dataProvider="{_tasks}"/>              ◁────── 13
      <s:HGroup width="100%">
        <s:Button label="Delete" width="100%" height="30"
          enabled="{taskList.selectedItem != null}"       ◁────── 14
          click="deleteSelectedTask()"/>
      </s:HGroup>
    </s:VGroup>
  </s:Panel>
</s:Application>
```

❶ We begin by creating an fx:Script element to hold ActionScript code inside a CDATA block.

❷ Next, we add imports, which make the classes accessible in this class.

❸ We then create a _tasks variable of type ArrayCollection, and initialize it to a new ArrayCollection. This variable is the source of a data binding in the List, so we need to mark it with the [Bindable] annotation.

❹ The createTask function calls the addItem method of the _tasks ArrayCollection with a new Task whose name is the value of the newTaskTI.text. This function has a void return value, meaning it returns nothing.

❺ The deleteSelectedTask function calls the removeItemAt method of the _tasks ArrayCollection, removing the task whose index is the taskList.selectedIndex.

❻ Next, we create a Panel whose title is "Todo List." It has a width and height of 100 percent, meaning it will take up the full width and height that are left after taking into account the padding of the parent application.

❼ The first component we create inside the Panel is a VGroup, which is a container for other components that lays out its children vertically.

❽ The first of these children is an HGroup, which is also a container of other user interface components and lays out its children horizontally. Inside the HGroup, we create a Label, a TextInput, and a Button.

❾ This is the New Task label.

❿ The TextInput has an id of newTaskTI. In MXML, the id property of a component becomes its variable name (the MXML file is a class, and the id is the name of a public member variable inside that class). If we don't provide an id for a component, Flex provides one for us—but then we don't know what it is, so we can't refer to the component in our code. Sometimes this is fine: we don't need to refer to the Button, so we don't bother giving it an id. Note that the newTaskTI calls createTask whenever it broadcasts the enter event.

⓫ We also modify the Create button to call createTask when it broadcasts its click event.

⓬ The taskList has a labelField of name (since that is the property of the Task that we want displayed).

⓭ The taskList has its dataProvider bound to the _tasks. This means that the List component displays a vertical list of items that are driven by data supplied from a data provider, in this case the Array-Collection _tasks. Specific properties of the members of the data provider object can be chosen as the values to display, in this example, the name property of the Task object is chosen for that role by being supplied as the value of the labelField attribute.

⓮ Finally, the Delete button has its enabled property bound to whether there's a non-null selectedItem in the taskList (thus preventing a user from trying to delete a nonexistent Task) and has its click event handled and trigger the deleteSelectedTask function. We only want the Delete button to be visibly available (as opposed to being grayed out and inactive) when the user has clicked on a specific item in the list. The selectedItem property of the list is bound to whatever item in the list is selected, and will be null if none are selected. So, we capitalize on this fact to control the enabled state of the Delete button.

➡ Key points

- Flex applications typically consist of many MXML and ActionScript components, which are stored in .mxml and .as files. These components are organized into packages.

- MXML is used for UI layout and ActionScript (both in MXML Script blocks and in ActionScript files) is used for behavior. You can even put ActionScript code (for example, function calls) inside the values of MXML attributes, such as `click="deleteSelectedTask()"`.

- These components communicate via data binding and by manually dispatching events.

SESSION 5 Spark, Halo, and Flex 4 namespaces

Before we go further, we should confront something that stares at you when you first look at a Flex 4 application: namespaces, and why we need three of them. To grasp this, we need to understand the story of Flex components.

Once upon a time (in Flex 1.0, 1.5, 2, and 3), all the components were something called "Halo" components, since they had a nice glow. (If my memory is correct, in Flex 1 and 1.5 this used to be green; in Flex 2 and 3 it was blue.) Anyway, since there was one set of components, they were all in the same namespace. In Flex 3, this namespace was `http://www.adobe.com/2006/mxml`, so Flex applications looked like this:

```
<?xml version="1.0" encoding="utf-8"?>
<mx:Application xmlns:mx="http://www.adobe.com/2006/mxml"
    layout="absolute">
    <mx:Button label="Hello World"/>
</mx:Application>
```

Simple, isn't it? One namespace, which gets assigned the prefix mx, letting you write things like mx:Button, mx:Application, and so forth. This

VERY OBSERVANT, ESPECIALLY THIS EARLY IN THE WORKSHOP. IT'S ACTUALLY NOT SO BAD. THERE'S A NAMESPACE FOR THE NEW "SPARK" COMPONENTS (WHICH GETS THE S PREFIX), A NAMESPACE FOR THE OLD "HALO" COMPONENTS (THIS GETS THE MX PREFIX), AND A NAMESPACE FOR CORE FLEX STUFF (THIS GETS THE. FX PREFIX).
THIS SEEMS COMPLEX, AND THERE IS A BIT OF PAIN IN LEARNING, BUT IT'S BETTER THAN WHAT ADOBE ORIGINALLY PROPOSED.

simplicity hid a big problem, however: the Halo components weren't easily "skinnable" by designers, meaning that their visual appearance couldn't be changed easily without lots of programming. To "skin" them beyond what you control with Cascading Style Sheets (CSS), you'd typically have to subclass them and do a lot of custom coding. Since Flash and Flex are making their way into a lot of design-oriented development shops like agencies, this kind of thing happens more than the average Java or .NET developer would expect. And nobody wants to be wrestling with overriding core Flex component behavior agency timetables and deadlines.

WOW, HOW BAD WAS THE ORIGINAL IDEA?

Fx PREFIXES. EVERYWHERE. YOU'D GO TO THE FxDentist FOR AN FxRootCanal. RYAN STEWART WOULD DRILL PERSONALLY!

IN LOLCAT TERMS, "DESIGN IN MIND" MEANS "I'M IN UR SDK, REWRITIN UR COMPONENTZ"

So, since Adobe understands designers better than most large companies, one of the themes Adobe had for Flex 4 is "Design in Mind." In marketing terms, this means that Adobe cares about designer-developer workflow and is striving to optimize it.

In this workshop session, we're going to see what a Flex 4 application using only Halo components looks like. We'll build the same application as the previous workshop session, a Todo List. This is useful since, as a Flex developer, you'll probably still need to use some Halo components on a daily basis (we'll go into which ones more in chapter 5). Those of you who have developed Flex 3 applications before will find this code very familiar.

session05/src/TodoList.mxml

```
<?xml version="1.0" encoding="utf-8"?>
<mx:Application                                          1
    xmlns:fx="http://ns.adobe.com/mxml/2009"            2
    xmlns:s="library://ns.adobe.com/flex/spark"
    xmlns:mx="library://ns.adobe.com/flex/halo">
<fx:Script>
<![CDATA[
```

```
  import mx.collections.ArrayCollection;
  import com.pomodo.model.Task;

  [Bindable]
  private var _tasks:ArrayCollection = new ArrayCollection();

  private function createTask():void {
    _tasks.addItem(new Task(newTaskTI.text));
  }

  private function deleteSelectedTask():void {
    _tasks.removeItemAt(taskList.selectedIndex);
  }
]]>
</fx:Script>
  <mx:Panel title="Todo List" width="100%" height="100%"        ◁————❸
    layout="vertical">
    <mx:HBox width="100%" verticalAlign="middle">
      <mx:Label text="New Task"/>
      <mx:TextInput id="newTaskTI" width="100%"
        enter="createTask()"/>
      <mx:Button label="Create" click="createTask()"/>
    </mx:HBox>
    <mx:List id="taskList" width="100%" height="100%"
      labelField="name"
      dataProvider="{_tasks}"/>
    <mx:ControlBar width="100%">
      <mx:Button label="Delete" width="100%" height="30"
        enabled="{taskList.selectedItem != null}"
        click="deleteSelectedTask()"/>
    </mx:ControlBar>
  </mx:Panel>
</mx:Application>
```

❶ For those who are new to Flex, the root tag is an mx:Application, since it is a Halo application. (If you look back at the previous workshop sessions, you'll see that the root tag we've been using has been s:Application [for a Spark application].)

❷ We create the three XML namespaces: First, the fx prefix for the core Flex namespace (http://ns.adobe.com/mxml/2009); second, the s prefix for the new Spark components namespace (library://ns.adobe.com/flex/spark); and third, the mx prefix for the old Halo components namespace (library://ns.adobe.com/flex/halo).

❸ Finally, we create a bunch of Halo components, like Panel, HBox, Label, List, and ControlBar. HBox and VBox are the Halo functional equivalent of HGroup and VGroup in Spark.

Next, we create a Task class that's identical to the Task class in workshop session 3.

session05/src/com/pomodo/model/Task.as

```
package com.pomodo.model {
    public class Task {
        [Bindable]
        public var name:String;

        public function Task(name:String = "") {
            this.name = name;
        }
    }
}
```

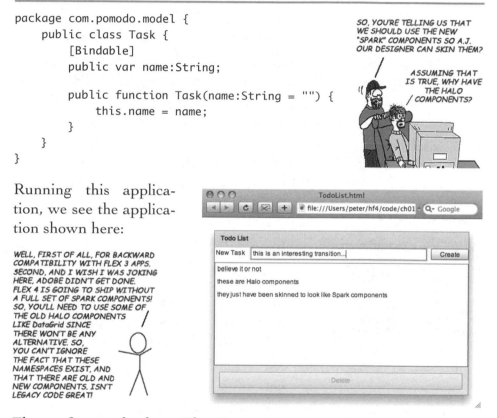

Running this application, we see the application shown here:

WELL, FIRST OF ALL, FOR BACKWARD COMPATIBILITY WITH FLEX 3 APPS. SECOND, AND I WISH I WAS JOKING HERE, ADOBE DIDN'T GET DONE. FLEX 4 IS GOING TO SHIP WITHOUT A FULL SET OF SPARK COMPONENTS! SO, YOU'LL NEED TO USE SOME OF THE OLD HALO COMPONENTS LIKE DataGrid SINCE THERE WON'T BE ANY ALTERNATIVE. SO, YOU CAN'T IGNORE THE FACT THAT THESE NAMESPACES EXIST, AND THAT THERE ARE OLD AND NEW COMPONENTS. ISN'T LEGACY CODE GREAT!

Those of you who have Flex 3 experience may be surprised: this doesn't look like a Halo application in Flex 3! The reason for this is simple: Adobe understands that you need to mix and match Halo and Spark components in Flex 4, so they changed the style of the Halo components in Flex 4 to match the Spark components.

BUT WON'T THE NEW COMPONENTS LOOK A LOT DIFFERENT THAN THE OLD ONES FROM FLEX 3?

YEAH, EXCEPT ADOBE IS SKINNING THE OLD ONES TO MATCH...

➤➤ **Key points**

- Flex 4 applications typically use three XML namespaces, since Flex 4 is introducing an entirely new set of components (the Spark components).

- The old school Halo components are what were used in Flex 1-3. They have the `mx` prefix by convention, since that's what was used in Flex 1 through 3. The namespace for the Halo components is `library://ns.adobe.com/flex/halo`. You still need to use the Halo components where there are no Spark equivalents yet, such as `DataGrid`.

- The new Spark components use, by convention, an `s` prefix for the new namespace of `library://ns.adobe.com/flex/spark`. These components have "Design in Mind," which will allow designers and developers to work together in a more harmonious way.

- The `fx` prefix is for the core Flex namespace (`http://ns.adobe.com/mxml/2009`). This is for things like declarations, metadata, and script blocks—basically, for nonvisual language elements.

What's next?

GOING FROM THIS FAST-PACED INTRODUCTION TO LEARNING ACTIONSCRIPT 3 MAY SEEM A LITTLE DISAPPOINTING, BUT I'LL KEEP IT REALLY BRIEF AND ASSUME YOU KNOW HOW TO PROGRAM. I WON'T BORE YOU WITH AN INTRODUCTION TO OBJECT ORIENTED PROGRAMMING.

In this chapter we had a quick tour of Flex 4, got up and running, learned the basics of events and data binding, and even explored what the heck all these `xmlns` things mean. In the next chapter full of workshop sessions, we'll go a bit slower, learning ActionScript 3 and the Flex 4 fundamentals.

No, I won't bore you with an introduction to object-oriented programming; in this book I'm assuming you are a software developer already —just not a Flex one (yet).

2

ActionScript 3, XML, and E4X

f you don't know a decent amount of ActionScript 3, Flex 4 will always be a mystery. So in this chapter, you'll learn the basics of ActionScript 3. Once again, we'll build a series of self-contained workshop sessions. However, to minimize context switching we'll base them on a similar toy example. These workshop sessions will explain numerous concepts at once, since it's hard to explain arrays without involving looping, and vice versa. Also, we'll cover multiple concepts at once out of necessity: there are entire books devoted to learning ActionScript 3—and this is not one of those books.

PITR, THAT JOKE IS ABOUT 10 YEARS OLD. IF YOU WANT TO BE A COOL DESIGNER YOU NEED TO JOKE ABOUT TEH INTERWEBS AND CAT PICTURES.

Instead, we'll explore the basics of ActionScript 3 in five workshop sessions. This obviously will be a very high-level treatment, but you should absorb enough that you can use Flex 4 comfortably even if you've never seen ActionScript before.

ALSO, YOU GOT THE JOKE WRONG. YOU NEED TO INVERT SOMETHING THAT USUALLY HAPPENS, LIKE "PARTY FIND YOU", NOT COMBINE THREE THINGS THAT DON'T BELONG.

DID I SAY I CAN HAZ COMEDY LESSON? DO NOT WANT!

If you're an experienced Flex 3 developer who is just reading this book for the Flex 4 stuff, you can safely skip this chapter.

SESSION 6 Variables, functions, types, and scope

In this workshop session, we'll begin tackling the basics of ActionScript 3. These include variables, functions, and accessors and mutators (better known as getters and setters). These also include the types and access control namespace (commonly referred to as "scope") attributes (better known as public, protected, internal, and private) of these variables and functions. As always, you'll learn by doing. Let's start by creating a model package and a Task class inside it.

SO, I'M A DESIGNER... DO I REALLY NEED TO LEARN ACTIONSCRIPT 3?

IN THEORY, NO, SINCE YOU WILL BE ABLE TO USE FLASH CATALYST TO PRODUCE MXML.

HOWEVER, AS A DESIGNER, YOU INTERACT WITH DEVELOPERS ON A REGULAR BASIS, SO IT'S NICE TO LEARN ACTIONSCRIPT FOR EMPATHY. ALSO, SINCE YOU CAN USE FLASH CATALYST TO DO MORE, YOU MIGHT...

...END UP DOING A BIT OF AS3 CODING TO ENSURE YOUR CREATIVE VISION IS MORE CLOSELY FOLLOWED. BESIDES, THEN YOU CAN BE A "ROCK STAR", WHICH IS WEB 2.0 FOR "TALENTED", IT SEEMS.

sessionO6/src/model/Task.as

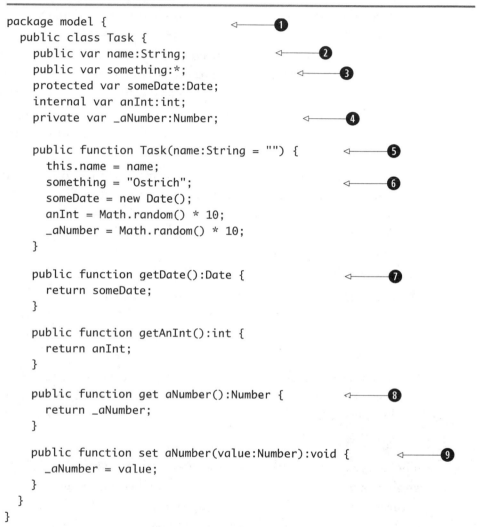

```
package model {
  public class Task {
    public var name:String;
    public var something:*;
    protected var someDate:Date;
    internal var anInt:int;
    private var _aNumber:Number;

    public function Task(name:String = "") {
      this.name = name;
      something = "Ostrich";
      someDate = new Date();
      anInt = Math.random() * 10;
      _aNumber = Math.random() * 10;
    }

    public function getDate():Date {
      return someDate;
    }

    public function getAnInt():int {
      return anInt;
    }

    public function get aNumber():Number {
      return _aNumber;
    }

    public function set aNumber(value:Number):void {
      _aNumber = value;
    }
  }
}
```

❶ The Task class is in the model package.

❷ Variables are created with declarations like public var name:String; that specify the access control (public), the variable name (name), and the type (String). Access control can be public, protected, internal, or private. (You can also use your own custom access control namespaces—if you're interested, see the "Packages and namespaces" section of Chapter 4 of Adobe's *Programming ActionScript*

3 book for details. Note that this language feature is almost never used when writing typical Flex applications; I'm only mentioning it here for completeness.)

❸ The special type * can be used to indicate any type. You can also skip the type declaration, but doing so produces compiler warnings. Type checking is your friend, so use explicit types when you can.

❹ These variables are examples of both primitives (`Boolean`, `int`, `uint`, `Number`, and `String`) and of core classes (such as `Date`) that don't need to be imported.

❺ The constructor function is used to initialize the object. Functions can take parameters, which can have default values. If a function parameter has a default value, the actual argument can be omitted. All functions except the constructor function can—and *should*—have return types.

❻ If something is untyped, it can be anything—even an ostrich.

❼ This `public` function returns a `Date` (`someDate`), which is `protected`. The return type of a function is specified after the argument list.

❽ This getter returns `_aNumber`. Note that the `function` keyword is followed by the `get` keyword.

❾ This setter sets `_aNumber` to `value`. All setter functions return void—that is, nothing. Note that the `function` keyword is followed by the `set` keyword. By convention, the parameter to a set function is always called `value`.

The access control of a variable determines who can access it. The choices are `public` (any class), `protected` (the class itself or subclasses), `internal` (classes in the same package) or `private` (the class itself). Unlike in Java, `protected` does *not* give access to classes in the same package.

We also encountered types in the `Task` model earlier, such as the `String` in `public var name:String`. Type checking is done at both compile time and runtime. Compile-time type checking is disabled when either the type is omitted (which produces a compiler warning in Strict mode) or explicitly left unspecified with the * (which prevents the compiler warning). To avoid type errors at runtime it's best to do as much compile-time type checking as possible, so it's a good idea to type your variables.

(When I work with Ruby programmers on Flex projects, I don't even tell them that compile-time type checking is optional!)

There are two kinds of types that we encountered earlier. The primitive types in ActionScript are `Boolean` (true/false), `int` (a 32-bit signed integer), `uint` (a 32-bit unsigned integer), `Number` (a 64-bit floating point), and `String` (which stores text). There are also a number of "core classes," which are `Object`s but that are imported automatically by the compiler so you don't need to add import statements yourself. The core classes include `Object` (everything that isn't primitive is an `Object`), `Array`, `Date`, `Error` (for exceptions), `Function` (which are called methods when they're part of objects), `RegExp`, `XML`, and `XMLList`. As we'll see later in this chapter, ActionScript 3 features outstanding XML support using something called E4X.

Now that we've created the `Task` class, let's use it. We'll build a top-level Flex app called Tester to do just that.

session06/src/Tester.mxml

```
<?xml version="1.0" encoding="utf-8"?>
<s:Application
  xmlns:fx="http://ns.adobe.com/mxml/2009"
  xmlns:s="library://ns.adobe.com/flex/spark"
  xmlns:mx="library://ns.adobe.com/flex/halo"
  width="100%" height="100%"
  initialize="init()">
<fx:Script>
<![CDATA[
  import com.pomodo.model.Task;                    <--- ❶

  private function init():void {
    var task:Task = new Task("learn ActionScript 3");   <--- ❷
    outputTA.text = "Name: " + task.name + "\n" +       <---
      "Something: " + task.something + "\n" +           ❸
      "Date: " + task.getDate() + "\n" +
      "Int: " + task.getAnInt() + "\n" +
      "Number: " + task.aNumber;
    task.something = 5;                                 ❹
    outputTA.text += "\nNow something is: " + task.something;  <---
    task.aNumber = 3.14;                                <--- ❺
```

```
    outputTA.text += "\nNow aNumber is: " + task.aNumber;
  }
]]>
</fx:Script>
  <s:TextArea id="outputTA" width="100%" height="100%"/>
</s:Application>
```

❶ Our Task class isn't a "core class," so it needs to be imported using import.

❷ Create a new Task object, passing the name into the constructor.

❸ We assign the text property of the outputTA TextArea with a String showing the state of the Task. For non-public variables we use the functions. Note that the aNumber getter is accessed using the same property syntax as variables like name and something. (We will cover TextArea in greater detail in subsequent chapters; for now, just think of it as a big rectangular component that can edit text.)

❹ Since something is untyped, it can go from being the String "Ostrich" to the number 5.

❺ Assign 3.14 to _aNumber via the aNumber setter. Note that this property assignment looks the same as the assignment to the something variable of the Task object.

Let's see what this does. Run the Tester app; you'll see a screen like the following—except your Date will almost certainly be different and your random number will (almost!) certainly be different.

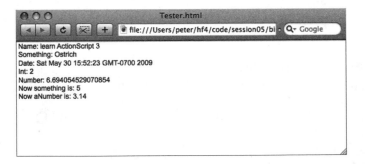

That's it! Now that we've seen the basics of variables, functions, access control, and types, we can move on to the next workshop session where we play with Objects, Arrays, and control flow (branching and looping).

➤➤ **Key points**

- ○ Variables are declared with var.

- ○ Functions are declared with function.

- ○ All functions can take arguments, and all functions except the constructor function can return values.

- ○ If a non-constructor function doesn't return anything, specify that it returns nothing by using the void keyword.

- ○ Variables and functions can (and should) have a public, private, protected, or internal access level. (I say *should* since by default you'll get a warning unless you specify the access level. Just do it.)

- ○ Getters and setters can be used to provide property-style access to private variables that looks indistinguishable to a variable from the outside world but that can do other interesting things.

SESSION 7 *Objects, Arrays, Collections, and Looping*

In this workshop session, we'll learn more ActionScript. We take a fast-paced tour of the Object class, anonymous objects, Array and ArrayCollection, branching (if/else, switch, and the ternary operator) and looping (for, for each, for in, while, do while). The assumption here is that you've seen arrays, if statements, and loops before—just not in Action-Script. Almost any popular programming language has them, and they're just as unsurprising here as elsewhere. (If you need a more thorough treatment of ActionScript 3 than this chapter provides, I highly recommend the *Programming ActionScript 3* PDF that comes with the Flex 3 documentation at http://livedocs.adobe.com/flex/3/progAS_flex3.pdf. Once it's updated for Flex 4, presumably later in 2009, there will be a newer URL. Again, Google is your friend here.) Furthermore, we'll do all this in one function inside one carefully constructed code example, shown next.

session07/src/Tester.mxml

```
<?xml version="1.0" encoding="utf-8"?>
<s:Application
  xmlns:fx="http://ns.adobe.com/mxml/2009"
  xmlns:s="library://ns.adobe.com/flex/spark"
  xmlns:mx="library://ns.adobe.com/flex/halo"
  width="100%" height="100%"
  initialize="init()">
<fx:Script>
<![CDATA[
  import mx.collections.ArrayCollection;

  private function init():void {
    var foo:Object = new Object();                              ← ❶
    var house:Object = {country: "Canada", province: "BC",
      city: "Vancouver"};
    var ary:Array = [foo, house, 1];
    ary.push("last");
    ary.unshift(true);

    var output:String = "Join:\n" + ary.join(", ") + "\n";      ← ❷
    output += "for loop over Array:\n";
    for (var i:int = 0; i < ary.length; i++) {                  ← ❸
      output += ary[i] + (i == ary.length - 1 ? "\n" : ", ");
    }
    output += "for loop over ArrayCollection:\n";
    var ac:ArrayCollection = new ArrayCollection(ary);          ← ❹
    for (var j:int = 0; j < ac.length; j++) {
      output += ac.getItemAt(j);
      switch(j) {
        case ac.length - 1:
          output += "\n";
          break;
        default:
          output += ", ";
          break;
      }
    }
    output += "for each loop over ArrayCollection:\n";
    var k:int = 0;
    for each (var item:Object in ac) {                          ← ❺
      output += item;
      if (k != ac.length - 1) {
```

```
      output += ", ";
    } else {
      output += "\n";
    }
    k++;
  }
  output += "for in over Object properties:\n"                    ←———— ⑥
  for (var key:String in house) {
    output += house[key] + ", ";
  }
  outputTA.text = output;
}
]]>
</fx:Script>
  <s:TextArea id="outputTA" width="100%" height="100%"/>
</s:Application>
```

❶ Objects can be constructed with either the new Object() syntax or by creating an anonymous Object using curly braces. Don't confuse this use of curly braces with data binding: both use curly braces ({}), but the compiler figures out what you are doing based on context. Similarly, Arrays can be constructed using the new Array() syntax or by using square brackets, [].

❷ Arrays have a join function that's useful for producing Strings without the need for a tedious loop. Arrays also have a map function, which is useful for functional programming–style code. Note that push adds something to the end of an Array, while unshift adds something to the beginning of an Array.

❸ ActionScript 3 has a standard for loop, as well as while and do while loops, which work the same way they do in every other language. Note the use of the ternary a ? b : c operator. I use int rather than uint as my loop index since that's the typical convention—while some people may complain that you should use uint since the loop indexes can't be negative, using int runs slightly faster. Also, I've never accidentally gotten a negative loop index while looping, so using uint is pedantic.

❹ Flex code often uses an ArrayCollection, which is in the mx.collections package. The ArrayCollection is more suitable for data binding than Array is, and Flex is all about data binding. This example shows that looping over an ArrayCollection is similar to an Array, except the getItemAt(index) method is used instead of the someArray[index] subscript notation. This example also shows the switch/case statement, which is used for multiway branching. Finally, note something very subtle: I used j and not i for my loop index variable, since I had already used a loop index variable i earlier in the function and since *variables inside a function are all in the same scope.* Yes, you read that correctly: the for loop does *not* create its own variable scope. (This is fairly atypical among programming languages, so be careful here!)

❺ ActionScript 3 has a for each ... in loop, which iterates over the *values* in a collection. This example also shows the standard if/else statement.

❻ ActionScript 3 has a for ... in loop, which iterates over the *keys* in a collection (or in an Object). These keys can be used to get the values, as shown here.

Running this example we, see the following screen.

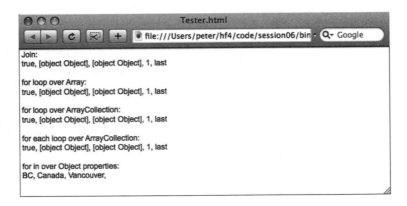

That's it!

➤➤ Key points

- ◎ Objects can be constructed with the new Object() or {key1: value1 , ... } syntax.

- ActionScript features the ternary operator, if/else, and switch statement, as well as the for, while, and do while loops you use all the time.
- ActionScript features for ... in and for each ... in loops.
- Flex often uses ArrayCollections to wrap Arrays and play nicely with data binding. Iterating over these ArrayCollections is straightforward.

SESSION 8 Interfaces, casting, is, and as

Having explored the basics of objects in ActionScript 3 in the previous two sessions, we'll now dive deeper in this workshop session and discuss interfaces, casting, and the is and as operators. After this, and our discussion of inheritance in the next workshop session, we'll have a good handle on the basics of objects in ActionScript.

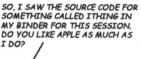

SO, I SAW THE SOURCE CODE FOR SOMETHING CALLED ITHING IN MY BINDER FOR THIS SESSION. DO YOU LIKE APPLE AS MUCH AS I DO?

Briefly, an interface is a contract (that is, a set of methods) that a class must honor if it implements the interface. The advantage of interfaces is that it lets you write more

NO, IT IS JUST A CONVENTION TO USE THE LETTER I FOR INTERFACE...

reusable code that's more abstracted and less coupled to implementation details. If you're familiar with interfaces from languages such as Java, you'll be happy to know that they work pretty much the same way in ActionScript 3. (Unfortunately, unlike Java, you can't add constants to ActionScript 3 interfaces.) Also, ActionScript 3 interfaces have support for property getters and setters, which is important since

I IS FOR INTERFACE. I LIKE IT... SOUNDS LIKE A SUE GRAFTON NOVEL.

otherwise they'd be virtually useless given how property-centric Flex is. (Although, unfortunately, you can't implement an interface and use a public var in the place of the getters and setters, which would have been a nice shortcut in trivial cases.) Understanding how to use interfaces will let us write more elegant code that's more flexible and less tied to one specific implementation.

In this session we'll create an IThing interface, which will be implemented by Task and Project classes. I use an agile project management tool called Pivotal Tracker every day, so I think about Tasks having "story points," which indicates how much work a Task should take. Since the number of story points in a project is the sum of its Tasks, we can put the points into the IThing interface and show a somewhat meaningful example.

session08/src/model/IThing.as

```
package model {
  public interface IThing {
    function get name():String;                    ← ❶
    function set name(value:String):void;
    function getPoints():int;                      ← ❷
  }
}
```

❶ Property get and set functions can go in an interface.

❷ Normal functions can go in an interface as well.

Note that no access control specifier is needed (or permitted), since all functions in an interface are public.

Next, we create a Task class that implements IThing.

session08/src/model/Task.as

```
package model {
  public class Task implements IThing {            ← ❶
    private var _name:String;
    public var points:int;
    public var due:Date;                                          ❷
    public static const ONE_DAY_IN_MSEC:Number = 24*60*60*1000;  ←
```

```
      public function Task(name:String = "") {
        this.name = name;
        due = new Date();
        due.setTime(due.getTime() + ONE_DAY_IN_MSEC);
      }
      public function getPoints():int {                    ⟵————— ❸
        return points;
      }
      public function get name():String {
        return _name;
      }
      public function set name(value:String):void {
        _name = value;
      }
    }
}
```

❶ Task implements IThing. Note that the use of underscores for private instance variables is a convention, not a language requirement. For a list of many useful Flex coding conventions see http://opensource.adobe.com/wiki/display/flexsdk/Coding+Conventions.

❷ The static keyword means that it belongs to the class itself; that is, it's independent of the instances of this class. The const keyword means that it's a constant, not a variable. (I used multiplication instead of just the result to be more readable. Note that the Date#getTime() method returns a Number, not an int.)

❸ Note that the method signatures match the interface, meaning the class must provide an implementation of the methods defined in the interface.

Next, we create a Project class that also implements IThing.

session08/src/model/Project.as

```
package model {
  import mx.collections.ArrayCollection;

  public class Project implements IThing {          ⟵————— ❶
    private var _name:String;
    public var tasks:ArrayCollection;
```

```
      public function Project(name:String = "") {
        this.name = name;
        tasks = new ArrayCollection();
      }
      public function get name():String {
        return _name;
      }
      public function set name(value:String):void {
        _name = value;
      }
      public function getPoints():int {                    ←———————— ❷
        var pointsTotal:int = 0;
        for each (var task:Task in tasks) {
          pointsTotal += task.points;
        }
        return pointsTotal;
      }
    }
  }
}
```

❶ Project implements IThing.

❷ The getPoints method calculates the points based on the tasks in the project.

Finally, we develop a Tester app that creates some Tasks and Projects and shows how they can be treated as IThings. It also illustrates the use of the is and as keywords.

session08/src/Tester.mxml

```
<?xml version="1.0" encoding="utf-8"?>
<s:Application
  xmlns:fx="http://ns.adobe.com/mxml/2009"
  xmlns:s="library://ns.adobe.com/flex/spark"
  xmlns:mx="library://ns.adobe.com/flex/halo"
  width="100%" height="100%"
  initialize="init()">
<fx:Script>
<![CDATA[
  import mx.collections.ArrayCollection;
  import model.Task;
  import model.Project;
  import model.IThing;
```

```
    private function init():void {
      var project1:Project = new Project("project 1");        ◄——————①
      var project2:Project = new Project("project 2");
      var task1:Task = new Task("task 1");
      task1.points = 3;
      var task2:Task = new Task("task 2");
      task2.points = 1;
      project1.tasks = new ArrayCollection([task1, task2]);   ◄——————②
      var things:ArrayCollection = new ArrayCollection([
        task1, task2, project2]);
      things.addItemAt(project1, 2);             ◄——————③
      var output:String = "";
      for each (var thing:IThing in things) {         ◄——————④
        output += thing.name + " (points: " + thing.getPoints() + ")";
        if (thing is Task) {                   ◄——┐
          var task:Task = Task(thing);             ⑤
          output += ", due: " + task.due;
        }
        var project:Project = thing as Project;        ◄——————⑥
        if (project != null) {
          output += ", " + project.tasks.length + " tasks";
        }
        output += "\n";
      }
      outputTA.text = output;
    }
]]>
</fx:Script>
  <s:TextArea id="outputTA" width="100%" height="100%"/>
</s:Application>
```

❶ We start by creating a couple of Projects and Tasks.

❷ The literal Array syntax can be used to create the argument to the ArrayCollection constructor, which takes an Array.

❸ Note the use of addItemAt to put a project into the ArrayCollection.

❹ We can loop over the ArrayCollection of Tasks and Projects and treat each of them as IThings.

❺ The is operator returns true if the thing is a Task (or a subclass of Task). If it is a Task, we can safely cast the thing to a Task using the Task(thing) syntax. Note that this is Task(thing) not (Task)thing, unlike in some other languages.

6 The as operator can be used safely where casting might blow up (if the object was the wrong type). If the type doesn't match, it just returns null. So, we use a null check.

Running this app produces the following output:

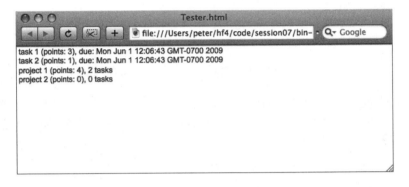

Note that Task and Project objects both show their number of points, which is done generically for IThings. However, the Tasks also show when they're due using code that only executes for Task objects (with the is check), and the Projects show how many Tasks they contain using code that only executes for Project objects (with the as and null checks).

That's it!

➤ Key points

- Interfaces can be used to specify a contract that objects must implement, in terms of public functions and getter and setter functions.

- The is keyword can be used to test whether an object is an instance of a class (which includes a subclass of that class).

- Casting can be used for explicit type conversion. Be careful, though, since if you cast and get it wrong, your program will explode. Guarding a cast with an is check is a good way to be careful—and is preferable to instanceof, which is an old way of doing this test that we won't discuss in this book.

- The as keyword lets you cast safely without an is test, and returns null if the type doesn't match. Of course, then you need to test for null...

SESSION 9 Inheritance

In this workshop session, you'll learn about inheritance. Inheritance is the "is a" kind of reuse, in which one "child" class is a subclass of a "parent" class (or superclass), and has all of its parent's properties and adds or overrides its own. The Flex framework has an extensive class hierarchy, defined (as all class hierarchies are) by inheritance.

The IThing interface and Tester application are unchanged from session 7. The Tester application is fairly long, so I won't show it again. To refresh your memory, here's the IThing interface:

session09/src/model/IThing.as

```
package model {
  public interface IThing {
    function get name():String;
    function set name(value:String):void;
    function getPoints():int;
  }
}
```

Now, one thing you might have noticed in the previous session was that there was duplicate code for setting the name. So, let's fix that. Let's create a Thing class that implements the common code for all Things, and that will throw an Error for functionality that must be implemented by subclasses. (If you're wondering "Why not just make an abstract class?" the simple answer is that abstract classes don't exist in ActionScript 3. So, this is how you fake it.)

session09/src/model/Thing.as

```
package model {
  public class Thing implements IThing {          ←——— ❶
    protected var _name:String;                   ←—
    public function Thing(name:String = "") {      ❷
```

```
      this.name = name;
    }
    public function getPoints():int {
      throw new Error("Unimplemented getPoints method");
    }
    public function set name(value:String):void {
      _name = value;
    }
    public function get name():String {
      return _name;
    }
  }
}
```

❸

❹

- ❶ Thing implements IThing.
- ❷ Thing has a protected _name variable. When building something you intend to be subclassed, you can use protected instead of private if you want to allow subclasses to have more access to the internals of the parent class. Or, you can take the approach of making the variable private and providing get/set methods, in order to ensure that subclasses access variables the same way as the outside world.
- ❸ Thing throws an Error if getPoints() isn't overridden. An Error is the ActionScript 3 version of an exception.
- ❹ Thing defines the get and set functions for name.

Now we're going to create Task and Project classes that extend Thing and thus implement IThing by inheritance. You can modify the code from the previous session, or create new code if you're creating different projects for each session.

session09/src/model/Task.as

```
package model {
  public class Task extends Thing {                              ⟵  ❶
    public var points:int;                          ⟵  ❷
    public var due:Date;
    public static const ONE_DAY_IN_MSEC:Number = 1000*60*60*24;

    public function Task(name:String = "") {
      super(name);
```

```
      due = new Date();
      due.setTime(due.getTime() + ONE_DAY_IN_MSEC);
    }
    public override function getPoints():int {            ◁——————— ❸
      return points;
    }
  }
}
```

❶ Task extends Thing (which implements IThing).

❷ Task has a points variable.

❸ Task overrides the getPoints function from Thing with the override keyword. This keyword is mandatory.

Next, we create a Project class that also extends Thing and thus implements IThing.

session09/src/model/Project.as

```
package model {
  import mx.collections.ArrayCollection;

  public class Project extends Thing {             ◁——————— ❶
    public var tasks:ArrayCollection;

    public function Project(name:String = "") {
      super(name);
      tasks = new ArrayCollection();
    }
    public override function getPoints():int {      ◁      ❷
      var pointsTotal:int = 0;
      for each (var task:Task in tasks) {
        pointsTotal += task.points;
      }
      return pointsTotal;
    }
  }
}
```

❶ The Project class also extends the Thing class.

❷ The Project class also overrides the getPoints function, summing the points of its tasks.

Running the Tester application results in the same output we saw earlier:

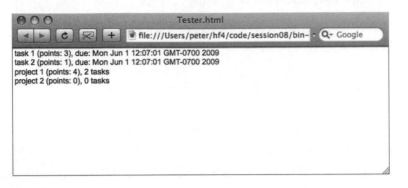

That's it for the "See Spot Run" stuff! In the next section we get to talk about XML, XMLListCollection, and E4X!

➤➤ Key points

- ◉ Inheritance is a useful way of preventing copy and paste code. (However, the older and more cynical I get, the more I prefer composition.)

- ◉ To subclass a class, use the extends keyword.

- ◉ When overriding a function, use the override keyword.

SESSION 10   E4X, XML, XMLList, and XMLListCollections

The previous four sessions showed the basics of ActionScript 3, which resemble the basics of any object-oriented programming language. Frankly, you may have been a little bored. Well, after my many years of software development and writing experience, I know the surefire way to cure boredom: XML.

Actually, in all seriousness, the way that Flex and ActionScript 3 support XML is pretty cool. Or, if you don't think it's cool, at least admit it's not as uncool as it is everywhere else!

In this workshop session, you'll learn how to use XML in Flex. This includes learning the built-in XML and XMLList types, as well as Flex's XMLListCollection. As a bonus, we'll learn how to sort collection classes that, like

ListCollectionView IMPLEMENTS BOTH IList AND ICollectionView, SO YOU CAN PASS IT AND ITS SUBCLASSES TO FUNCTIONS THAT TAKE EITHER AS A PARAMETER.

AND BOTH ArrayCollection AND XMLListCollection EXTEND ListCollectionView, SO THEY IMPLEMENT THOSE INTERFACES BY INHERITANCE. THIS IS THE FAMED "IS-A" TYPE OF REUSE, NOT "HAS-A" WHICH IS FOR COMPOSITION. THERE. THAT'S ALL THE O-O THEORY FOR THIS SESSION, HONEST...

XMLListCollection and ArrayCollection, extend ListCollectionView and implement ICollectionView: this is a Flex book after all.

What we're going to do is create a new Tester app. This one will be stand-alone. Its entire purpose in life will be to create some XML and then do some stuff to it.

session10/src/Tester.mxml

```
<?xml version="1.0" encoding="utf-8"?>
<s:Application
  xmlns:fx="http://ns.adobe.com/mxml/2009"
  xmlns:s="library://ns.adobe.com/flex/spark"
  xmlns:mx="library://ns.adobe.com/flex/halo"
  width="100%" height="100%"
  initialize="init()">
<fx:Script>
```

```
<![CDATA[
    import mx.collections.XMLListCollection;          ◄────────❶
    import mx.collections.Sort;
    import mx.collections.SortField;

  private var _projectsXML:XML =                      ◄────────❷
<projects>
  <project id="1" name="Proj1">
    <task id="1">
      <name>Understand E4X</name>
      <notes>cool, for XML anyway</notes>
    </task>
    <task id="2">
      <name>Learn XMLList</name>
      <notes>simple</notes>
    </task>
  </project>
  <project id="2" name="Proj2">
    <task id="3">
      <name>Learn XMLListCollection</name>
    </task>
    <task id="4">
      <name>Get a coffee</name>
      <notes>very necessary</notes>
    </task>
  </project>
</projects>;

  private function init():void {
    var output:String = "";
    output += "Full XML:\n" + _projectsXML;
    output += "\n\nUsing E4X and XMLList:\n";                           ❸
    output += _projectsXML.project[0].task[0].name + "\n";      ◄──────
output += _projectsXML.project.(@name=="Proj2").task.(@id==3).name;
    var projects:XMLList = _projectsXML.children();         ◄──────
    for each (var project:XML in projects) {                       ❹
      output += "Project: " + project.@name + "\n";        ◄──────
      for each (var task:XML in project.task) {                    ❺
        output += "  Task " + task.@id + ": " + task.name;
        if (task.hasOwnProperty('notes')) {              ◄──────
          output += " (" + task.notes + ")";                      ❻
        }
        output += "\n";
```

```
        }
      }
      output += "\nLearning XMLListCollection and Sorting:\n"
      var allTasks:XMLListCollection = new XMLListCollection(       ⟵
        _projectsXML.descendants("task"));                              ❼
      var sort:Sort = new Sort();
      sort.fields = [new SortField("name",true)];          ⟵
      allTasks.sort = sort;                                      ❽
      allTasks.refresh();
      for each (var sortedTask:XML in allTasks) {          ⟵
        output += sortedTask.name + "\n";                       ❾
      }
      outputTA.text = output;
    }
  ]]>
</fx:Script>
  <s:TextArea id="outputTA" width="100%" height="100%"/>
</s:Application>
```

❶ XMLListCollection, Sort, and SortField are Flex framework classes so they must be imported.

❷ We create literal XML and assign it to a variable of type XML. Yes, this is XML inside a CDATA tag inside XML. Note that ActionScript natively understands XML literals; there is no special syntax required when using XML literal expressions.

❸ You can use E4X (an acronym for ECMAScript 4 XML; ActionScript is based on ECMAScript) to get child nodes by index or by searches on attribute values such as @name=="Proj2".

❹ Getting the children of an XML object gets an XMLList, which can be iterated on with a for each loop.

❺ E4X, attribute, and child element values can be retrieved with dot (.) syntax. For an attribute value, just add the @ prefix.

❻ You can use the hasOwnProperty function to check whether a property (element or attribute) exists.

❼ We construct a new XMLListCollection of *all* the tasks by getting all the descendant elements of the root node that are named task. Note that this does not include text nodes, XML comments, processing instructions or attributes.

We then create a new `Sort` object and add a `SortField` of `name` (with `caseInsensitive` set to `true` with the second parameter to the constructor). This `Sort` is then assigned to the `allTasks` collection and then the collection's `refresh()` method is called to update the collection to be sorted by the `Sort`.

 Now that the collection is sorted, we can iterate through the sorted collection and output the names.

Run the app; you'll see the following screen:

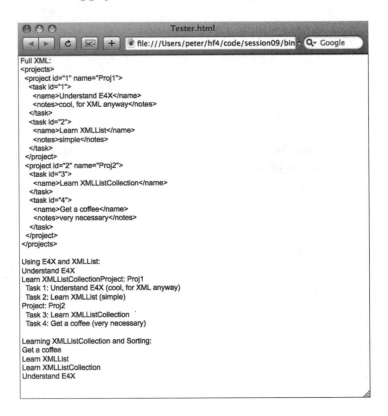

Note the nice display of the projects and the tasks they contain, which was produced by the nested loops. Also, note that the `XMLListCollection` is sorted: "Get a coffee" comes before "Understand E4X," as it should!

➠ Key points

- E4X, which stands for ECMAScript for XML, is a great way to handle XML. You'll never want to touch the DOM or have SAX again.

- `XMLListCollection` is a nice, friendly way to work with `XMLList`, and lets you sort the data using the same approach that can be used with any Flex collection, such as `ArrayCollection`, that implements `ListCollectionView`. We will see `ArrayCollections` and XML used extensively in the book, so don't worry if this seems a bit like drinking from a firehose. That's the intent; I want to get back to Flex as fast as possible.

- `XML` and `XMLList` are native types in ActionScript 3 and don't need to be imported.

What's next?

What's next? Simple: we're going back to Flex!

Well, that's kind of a misnomer: since all Flex 4 programming is done in ActionScript 3, we never really left: writing MXML typically involves writing nested ActionScript in `CDATA` tags, and even the MXML itself is all translated behind the scenes by the MXML compiler into ActionScript 3 before being compiled again.

But you probably didn't buy this book to learn about interfaces or E4X, so we rushed through this chapter so that we could get to the cool stuff as soon as possible. Now that we've made it through this chapter, and you learned a bit of ActionScript along the way, we'll slow down a bit and do what we came here to do: learn Flex 4, specifically, the shiny Flex 4 that impressed you enough to buy the book in the first place.

Specifically, in chapters 3 and 4 we'll focus on the new Spark primitives and components that you use daily in Flex 4: text controls, buttons, combo boxes, lists, and so forth. In chapter 5 we'll explain the Halo components you still need to know about. In chapter 6 we'll take a deep dive into formatting and validation, which hasn't changed much from Flex 3 but that's still essential knowledge for any Flex developer. Finally, in chapter 7 we'll build the Twitter + Yahoo! Maps example that the entire interweb is buzzing about. In all these chapters, however, your knowledge of ActionScript 3 will be both used and deepened.

3

Hello Spark: primitives, components, FXG and MXML graphics, and even video

In this chapter, you'll start learning Spark, which is the new set of components, containers, and graphics primitives in Flex 4. This will be a "how-to" chapter: we'll save diving into the Spark component model until the next chapter (which discusses view states, containers, CSS styling, and skinning). This chapter provides enough examples of using Spark that when it comes time to tackle the theory you'll have plenty of examples in your head.

THIS IS A HIGH-LEVEL TOUR OF THE SPARK COMPONENTS. ALSO, WE WILL BUILD AN "ONLY CONNECT" GAME, SO YOUR LIFE AS A PROGRAMMER WILL FINALLY BE COMPLETE.

In four of the five workshop sessions in this chapter, we'll build a fairly small, self-contained Tester.mxml app that has all the code in the example. In session 14, however, I'll mix things up a little: we'll build an "Only Connect" game (that bears strong resemblance to a certain trademarked game). We'll start with a game board that I drew in Adobe Illustrator and saved as FXG. (I'm providing the FXG file I created, so you don't need to have Adobe Illustrator.) We'll then build a fully functioning game based on this FXG, before refactoring it and then adding logic for detecting victory. The victory detection logic is more complex code than you saw in the previous chapter, so if you're new to ActionScript 3 it will be good to read through it. (And if you're a "rock star" developer, you can refactor my code to be a lot more efficient.)

Session 14 is pretty long, so after we finish it, we'll do a toy example in session 15, in which we build the UI (minus logging in and posting to Twitter) of the world's most narcissistic (fake) Twitter client. This will let us see how to play with the user's camera and video.

At the end of this chapter, you'll have a good understanding of the basics of the primitives and components that form the building blocks of a Flex application. Furthermore, you'll understand both how to create these manually and how to start using FXG generated by tools like Adobe Illustrator.

So, let's get started!

SESSION 11 Spark primitives

In this workshop session, we'll start work with the primitives that are the basic building block classes used by Spark components. (When I say "primitives" in this chapter, I mean Spark primitives, not ActionScript language primitive types like `int`.) These classes live in the `spark.primitives` package, except for the `Label` which lives in the `spark.components` package. (There used to be a `SimpleText` component in the `spark.primitives` package, but Adobe replaced it with the `spark.components.Label` class in Flex 4 Beta 2. This book went to press very soon after Flex 4 Beta 2 was released, but we updated it to Beta 2.) The classes in the `spark.primitives` package include `BitmapImage`, `Ellipse`, `Graphic`, `Line`, `Path`, `Rect`, `RichEditableText`, and `RichText`. We'll see `Graphic` and some of the other classes in session 14, and explore the rest of them now.

We'll build an app that looks like this:

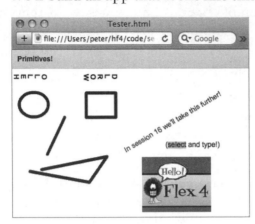

So, let's see the code.

session11/src/Tester.mxml

```
<?xml version="1.0" encoding="utf-8"?>
<s:Application
  xmlns:fx="http://ns.adobe.com/mxml/2009"
  xmlns:s="library://ns.adobe.com/flex/spark"
  xmlns:mx="library://ns.adobe.com/flex/halo"
  width="100%" height="100%">
<fx:Script><![CDATA[
  import mx.graphics.SolidColorStroke;

  private const _scs:SolidColorStroke =
    new SolidColorStroke(0x000000, 5, 1.0);                    ◄——— ❶

]]></fx:Script>
  <s:Panel width="100%" height="100%" title="Primitives!">           ❷
    <s:Ellipse x="12" y="39" width="50" height="40"            ◄———
      stroke="{_scs}"/>
    <s:Rect x="127" y="40" width="50" height="40" stroke="{_scs}"/> ❸
    <s:Line xFrom="90" yFrom="80" xTo="60" yTo="140"           ◄——— ❹
      stroke="{_scs}"/>
    <s:Path data="M30 168L132 186 162 144 50 165" stroke="{_scs}"/> ❺
    <s:Label="In session 16 we'll take this further!"          ◄———
      x="190" y="130" rotation="-30"/>                              ❻
    <s:RichText textRotation="rotate90" fontWeight="bold"      ◄——— ❼
      text="HELLO    WORLD"/>
    <s:RichEditableText text="(select and type!)" x="260" y="120"/> ❽
```

```
    <s:BitmapImage x="221" y="145" source="@Embed('HF4.png')"/>
  </s:Panel>
</s:Application>
```
9

❶ We create a `SolidColorStroke` that we assign to the various shapes. This stroke defines how the lines will appear for components that use it.

❷ The left eye is an `Ellipse`, which is a `FilledElement` (see inheritance hierarchy in a moment).

❸ The right eye is a `Rect`.

❹ The nose is a `Line`.

❺ The mouth is a `Path`. Note the nice short syntax, where M means "Move the pen," L means "Line from," and the rest are space-separated x and y values.

❻ The `Label` is not selectable with the cursor.

❼ The eyebrows are `RichText`. `RichText` is not selectable either, but it uses FXG so you can do stuff like rotate the text with the `textRota-tion` property.

❽ The `RichEditableText` is selectable and editable (try selecting it and typing).

❾ The `BitmapImage` class shows part of the book cover.

The following inheritance hierarchy shows how this all fits together. (The classes we are discussing in this chapter have shadows.)

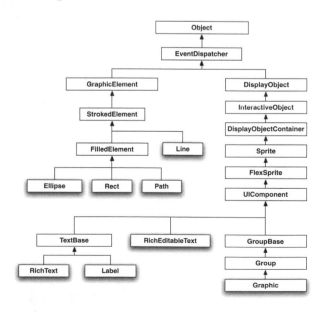

Note that `Ellipse`, `Rect`, and `Path` are all `FilledElement` subclasses, so they can have fills. Fills are the colors or patterns inside a shape. (You'll see this in session14 when we build the Only Connect game.) Since `FilledElement` and `Line` both extend `StrokedElement`, the `Ellipse`, `Rect`, `Path`, and `Line` can all have a stroke (the style of the line), as shown when we assigned the `SolidColorStroke` to each of them via data binding. Also note how the `RichEditableText` (which is selectable and editable) extends `UIComponent` directly, whereas `RichText` and `Label` extend `TextBase`. The `TextBase` and `RichEditableText` classes both extend `UIComponent`, which (eventually) extends `InteractiveObject`. The `InteractiveObject` class is an abstract base class for all the display object classes that the user can interact with using the keyboard and mouse.

In sum, the Spark primitives are organized into `GraphicElements` like `Ellipse` and `UIComponents` like `RichEditableText` and `Graphic`. As we'll see in session 14, since `Graphic` is a `UIComponent` it's easy to handle mouse events like clicks.

➤➤ Key points

- Spark primitives are the building blocks on which Spark components are built.
- Classes that can have a stroke extend `StrokedElement`; classes that can have a fill extend `FilledElement`.
- Classes that are interactive extend `InteractiveObject`.

SESSION 12 Simple Spark components

In this workshop session, we'll move up the food chain from the Spark primitives we discussed in the previous workshop session to the Spark components. We'll look at many of the most commonly used components in the spark.components package as we build a toy app that looks like this. These components are the building blocks of your application: without things like Buttons and TextInputs you wouldn't be able to build very many Flex apps! While the primitives are nice, you certainly don't want to reinvent the wheel.

Again, we'll start by examining the code, then provide the explanation and an inheritance hierarchy to show how it all fits together.

session12/src/Tester.mxml

```
<?xml version="1.0" encoding="utf-8"?>
<s:Application
  xmlns:fx="http://ns.adobe.com/mxml/2009"
  xmlns:s="library://ns.adobe.com/flex/spark"
  xmlns:mx="library://ns.adobe.com/flex/halo"
  width="100%" height="100%">
<fx:Script><![CDATA[
  [Bindable]                                          ❶
  private var _theory:String;                       ←

  [Bindable]                                          ❷
  private var _bread:Number = Number.NaN;           ←
]]></fx:Script>
<fx:Declarations>
  <s:RadioButtonGroup id="moralityRBG"/>
  <s:RadioButtonGroup id="restaurantRBG"             ❸
    selectedValue="{_theory.length % 2 == 0 ? 'smoking' : 'non'}"/> ◁
</fx:Declarations>
```

```
<s:Panel width="100%" height="100%" title="Simple Components!">
  <s:layout>
    <s:HorizontalLayout paddingLeft="5" paddingTop="5"/>
  </s:layout>
  <s:VGroup>
    <s:TextArea id="textArea" width="200" height="50"
      text="@{_theory}"/>                                        ❹
    <s:TextInput id="textInput" width="200" text="@{_theory}"/>
    <s:HSlider id="hSlider" minimum="0" maximum="11"
      liveDragging="true" width="200" value="@{_bread}"/>
    <s:VSlider id="vSlider" minimum="0" maximum="11"            ❺
      liveDragging="true" height="50" value="@{_bread}"/>
    <s:Button label="{_theory}" width="200"
      color="{alarmTB.selected ? 0xFF0000 : 0}"                 ❻
      click="_bread = Math.min(_theory.length, 11)"/>
    <s:CheckBox id="checkBox" selected="{_bread % 2 == 0}"
      label="even?"/>                                           ❼
  </s:VGroup>
  <s:VGroup>
    <s:RadioButton label="Good" value="good"
      group="{moralityRBG}"/>
    <s:RadioButton label="Evil" value="evil"
      group="{moralityRBG}"/>                                   ❽
    <s:RadioButton label="Beyond" value="beyond"
      group="{moralityRBG}"/>
    <s:RadioButton label="Smoking" value="smoking"
      group="{restaurantRBG}"/>
    <s:RadioButton label="Non-Smoking" value="non"
      group="{restaurantRBG}"/>                                 ❾
    <s:ToggleButton id="alarmTB" label="ALARM!"/>
    <s:NumericStepper id="numericStepper" value="@{_bread}"
      minimum="0" maximum="11" stepSize="1"/>                   ❿
    <s:Spinner id="spinner" value="@{_bread}"
      minimum="0" maximum="11" stepSize="1"/>
  </s:VGroup>
</s:Panel>
</s:Application>
```

❶ The String "_theory" is a variable that many of the components bind to.

❷ We create a _bread Number variable, and many of the components bind to it as well. Why did we call it _bread? Well, we're initializing it to NaN (Not a Number)… *(Yes, creating code examples at 3 a.m. makes my puns reach an all-time low!)*

❸ The `moralityRBG` and `restaurantRBG` RadioButtonGroups are used to create two sets of mutually exclusive choices, which the various `RadioButtons` are part of. Since the `RadioButtonGroups` aren't visual objects, they go in an `fx:Declarations` block.

❹ The `TextArea` and `TextInput` are multiline and single-line text components that have two-way bindings (with the @) to the `_theory` String.

❺ The `HSlider` and `VSlider` are both bound with two-way bindings to `_bread`.

❻ The `Button` has its label bound to the `_theory` String, and when clicked it assigns the length of the `_theory` String to the `_bread` variable (or 11 if the `_theory` String is longer). The `Math` class is a "core class," so we don't need to import it. Also note that the color property (which sets the text color) is bound to whether the `alarmTB` ToggleButton is selected (red if it is, black if it isn't).

❼ The `CheckBox` has its `selected` property bound to whether the `_bread` Number is even (selected) or odd (unselected). The % operator is for modulo, just like it is in virtually every other programming language worth knowing.

❽ The first three `RadioButtons` have their group set to the `moralityRBG`, so only one can be selected at once.

❾ This is the `alarmTB` ToggleButton, which has its `selected` boolean valued state determine the text color of the `Button` earlier.

❿ `NumericStepper` and `Spinner` are also two-way bound to `_bread`.

To understand where all this behavior comes, let's look at the inheritance hierarchy again. (To save space I'm drawing part of this hierarchy vertically and part of it horizontally.)

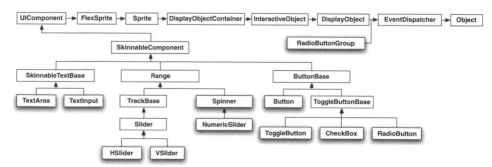

FLEX, AND MXML IN PARTICULAR, IS TRULY AMAZING: IT MAKES XML SEEM LIKE A TERSE WAY OF DOING SOMETHING!

The first thing to note is that all the components we've created are `SkinnableComponents`. You'll see what this means in more depth in the next chapter; for now, just know that it means we can customize their look easily.

Next, note that the `ToggleButton`, `CheckBox`, and `RadioButton` all extend `ToggleButtonBase`, so that's how they get their notion of whether they're selected. Also, see how the `NumericStepper` is just a subclass of `Spinner`; it adds the ability to type in a value yourself via its built-in `TextInput`. The `TextArea` and `TextInput` classes both extend `SkinnableTextBase` for some of their common functionality.

Finally, the `RadioButtonGroup` doesn't extend a visual component like `UIComponent`, but instead extends `EventDispatcher` directly, way up the inheritance hierarchy. This means the `RadioButtonGroup` isn't a visual component, which is why it's added to the `fx:Declarations` block (new to Flex 4)—where nonvisual components in MXML must go. (Note that `UIComponent` also happens to descend from `EventDispatcher`, but it and its ancestors add the behavior of being a visual component.)

➡ Key points

- The commonly used Spark components in the `spark.components` package all extend `Skinnable-Component` and can have their look customized.

- Use a `RadioButtonGroup` to ensure that only one `RadioButton` in the group can be selected.

IF NON-VISUAL COMPONENTS WEREN'T IN DECLARATIONS AND JUST IN THE MXML YOUR LAYOUT SPACING WOULD BE AFFECTED UNLESS THE MXML COMPILER DID SOMETHING SPECIAL...

SESSION 13 Data-driven Spark components (Lists)

In this workshop session, we'll continue our tour of Spark components by moving from the simple Spark components we saw in the previous session to a brief look at three data-driven components: List, DropDown-List, and ButtonBar. After we've done this, we'll build our Only Connect game in the next workshop session.

In this session we'll build the following application, which is a modern-day sanitized fairy tale creator.

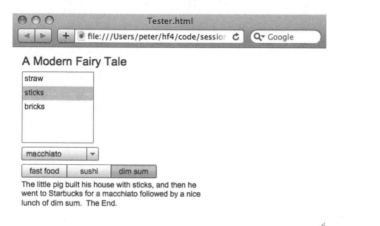

AS A PARENT, I'VE READ
ENOUGH OF THE
SANITIZED FAIRY
TALES THAT I
WOULDN'T BE
SURPRISED ONE DAY IF
THE THREE LITTLE PIGS
DID GO TO STARBUCKS
WITH THE WOLF!

So, let's take a look at the code.

session13/src/Tester.mxml

```
<?xml version="1.0" encoding="utf-8"?>
<s:Application
  xmlns:fx="http://ns.adobe.com/mxml/2009"
  xmlns:s="library://ns.adobe.com/flex/spark"
  xmlns:mx="library://ns.adobe.com/flex/halo"
  width="100%" height="100%">
<fx:Script><![CDATA[
  import spark.events.IndexChangeEvent;
  import mx.collections.ArrayCollection;

  [Bindable]
  private var _houseMaterials:ArrayCollection =
    new ArrayCollection(["straw", "sticks", "bricks"]);
```

```
  [Bindable]
  private var _coffees:ArrayCollection = new ArrayCollection([
    "drip coffee", "macchiato", "cappuccino", "latte"]);

  [Bindable]
  private var _lunches:ArrayCollection = new ArrayCollection([
    "fast food", "sushi", "dim sum"]);

  [Bindable]
  private var _pigChoice:String = "sticks";                    ← ➋

  [Bindable]
  private var _coffeeChoice:String = "macchiato";

  [Bindable]
  private var _lunchChoice:String = "dim sum";                 ➌
                                                               ←
  private function coffeeChanged(event:IndexChangeEvent):void {
    if (event.newIndex == -1) return;
    _coffeeChoice = _coffees.getItemAt(event.newIndex) as String;
  }
]]></fx:Script>
  <s:layout>
    <s:VerticalLayout paddingLeft="15" paddingTop="15"/>
  </s:layout>
  <s:Label text="A Modern Fairy Tale" fontSize="18"/>        ➍
  <s:List id="list" dataProvider="{_houseMaterials}"          ←
    selectedItem="{_pigChoice}"
    change="_pigChoice = list.selectedItem;"/>
  <s:DropDownList id="ddl" width="120"                    ←  ➎
    dataProvider="{_coffees}"
    selectedItem="{_coffeeChoice}"
    change="coffeeChanged(event)"/>
  <s:ButtonBar id="buttonBar" dataProvider="{_lunches}"   ← ➏
    selectedItem="{_lunchChoice}"
    click="_lunchChoice = buttonBar.selectedItem;"/>
  <s:Label width="300"                                       ➐
    text="The little pig built his house with {_pigChoice}, ←
and then he went to Starbucks for a {_coffeeChoice}
followed by a nice lunch of {_lunchChoice}.  The End."/>
</s:Application>
```

➊ We create ArrayCollections for the _houseMaterials, _coffees, and _lunches.

❷ We create `String` variables for the choices.

❸ The `coffeeChanged` function handles the `selectionChanged` event (of type `IndexChangeEvent`) broadcast when the user clicks the `DropDown-List` of coffee choices.

❹ The `List` shows the choices of `_houseMaterials` for the pig to use; its `selectedItem` is bound to the `_pigChoice`.

❺ The `DropDownList` shows the `_coffees` the pig can choose from, and its `selectedItem` is bound to the `_coffeeChoice`.

❻ The `ButtonBar` shows the `_lunches` the pig could choose from, and its `selectedItem` is bound to the `_lunchChoice`.

❼ The `Label` shows our sanitized fairy tale. Note how the `text` attribute in MXML can span multiple lines and contain multiple data bindings.

The following inheritance hierarchy diagram shows how related the `List`, `ButtonBar`, and `DropDownList` classes are.

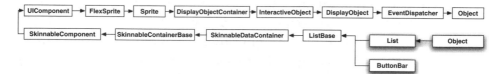

Note that the `DropDownList` is actually a subclass of `List`, which is a bit surprising. (For those of you who know Flex 3, the `DropDownList` replaces the Halo `ComboBox` class. The only thing the Halo `ComboBox` can do that `DropDownList` can't do is have its text be editable. However, I've always found the editable `ComboBox` text a bit flaky when trying to subclass it, so good riddance to `ComboBox` as far as I'm concerned.)

Finally, keep in mind that the `ButtonBar` can be used for navigation in conjunction with view states (which we'll see in the next chapter), to create the functionality of the

Halo TabNavigator or Halo ViewStack plus LinkBar combination, in which only one container component is shown based on which button the user selects.

➡ Key points

- ⊘ List, DropDownList, and ButtonBar all are descendants of ListBase, and the user can select one element (or in the case of List, multiple elements if the allowMultipleSelection property is set to true).

- ⊘ DropDownList subclasses List.

- ⊘ ButtonBar and view states can be used for navigation.

SESSION 14 FXG and MXML graphics—building a game

In the previous three workshop sessions, you learned how to code simple graphics manually and build small examples using Spark components. In this workshop session, we'll take a gigantic leap toward reality and build a real application: an Only Connect game. (We're going to call it Only Connect, since typically game names are trademarked.) You'll learn how the full workflow—from design to working Flex application—functions.

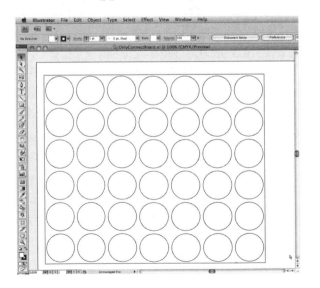

First, I drew the game board in Adobe Illustrator, since it can export FXG. After saving the Adobe Illustrator document (in an src/assets folder which I created in the session14 directory), I then also saved it as an FXG (Flash XML Graphics) document. We'll look at the source of that document momentarily.

If you have Adobe Illustrator and want to follow along (which is entirely optional, and I'm assuming you won't), be sure to deselect the Preserve Illustrator Editing Capabilities and Clip Content to Active Artboard check boxes, and then click OK. Also, don't create any extra groups for your circles.

When I saved the document as an FXG document, this is what it looked like:

session14/session14a/src/assets/OnlyConnectBoard.fxg

```
<?xml version="1.0" encoding="utf-8" ?>
<Graphic version="1.0" viewHeight="601" viewWidth="701"          ❶
xmlns="http://ns.adobe.com/fxg/2008">
  <Library/>
  <Group d:type="layer" d:userLabel="Layer 1"
xmlns:d="http://ns.adobe.com/fxg/2008/dt">
    <Rect x="0" y="0" width="700" height="600">            ❷
      <fill>
        <SolidColor color="#ffffff"/>
      </fill>
      <stroke>
        <SolidColorStroke caps="none" weight="1"
joints="miter" miterLimit="4"/>
      </stroke>
    </Rect>
    <Ellipse x="5" y="4" width="90" height="90">           ❸
      <fill>
        <SolidColor color="#ffffff"/>
      </fill>
      <stroke>
        <SolidColorStroke caps="none" weight="1"
joints="miter" miterLimit="4"/>
      </stroke>
    </Ellipse>
...a bunch of Ellipses...                                  ❹
    <Ellipse x="605" y="505" width="90" height="90">
      <fill>
        <SolidColor color="#ffffff"/>
      </fill>
      <stroke>
        <SolidColorStroke caps="none" weight="1"
joints="miter" miterLimit="4"/>
      </stroke>
    </Ellipse>
  </Group>
</Graphic>
```

❶ The root tag is a Graphic.

❷ The `Graphic` contains a `Group` tag, which contains a `Rect` for the outer rectangle.

❸ Each circle is an `Ellipse`.

❹ I'm skipping showing most of the `Ellipses` in order to save a tree; please see the code in the zip file on this book's website if you're interested.

If you were paying attention in session 11, these `Rect` and `Ellipse` elements should look familiar. In fact, the whole document looks similar to MXML. That's because MXML graphics are just FXG plus support for data binding!

So, you can save the FXG file from Illustrator and then load it in Flex Builder. Then just copy it and paste it into an MXML file, and with a couple minor tweaks you'll have a running app!

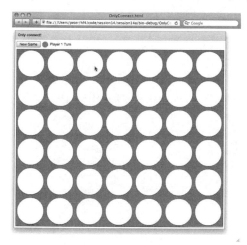

That's just awesome.

YOU SOUND LIKE A FANBOY.

I say this not as some kind of Adobe sychophant or "fanboy," but as someone who sees the value in rapid prototyping of UIs and putting this prototype in front of customers as early as possible. The fact that Adobe is pushing the FXG standard across their entire product line—Photoshop, Illustrator, Flash Catalyst, Flex—is very exciting.

So, in this session we'll go from that document to the following game in as few changes as possible. Then we'll refactor the code (since the FXG is repetitive), and then build game victory condition logic. In the process, you'll learn how to build visually complex Flex user interfaces using tools to do things that would be painful to do manually. (Yes, in this specific example, we could—and we will—also draw the game board using code. However, imagine if the game was Risk instead, and we wanted to use vector graphics instead of a bitmap image—I'd certainly rather draw the world in FXG than by writing ActionScript 3 code!)

The game that we're going to build looks like the following screens. Clicking on a column adds the chip of the player whose turn it is, as shown. The players take turns (no, there's no multiplayer—this is a workshop session!) until someone wins.

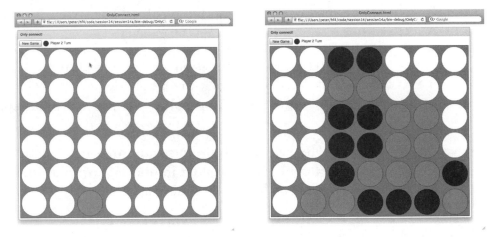

Note that we'll be adding victory detection later in this workshop session.

We'll create a main application called OnlyConnect and a BoardDisplay component based on the FXG. Let's start by creating the main application.

session14/session14a/src/OnlyConnect.mxml

```
<?xml version="1.0" encoding="utf-8"?>
<s:Application
  xmlns:fx="http://ns.adobe.com/mxml/2009"
  xmlns:s="library://ns.adobe.com/flex/spark"
  xmlns:mx="library://ns.adobe.com/flex/halo"
  xmlns:comp="components.*"
  width="100%" height="100%"
  initialize="board.newGame()">
  <fx:Script>
    <![CDATA[
      import mx.graphics.SolidColor;

      private function getColor(playerOneTurn:Boolean):SolidColor {
        return new SolidColor(playerOneTurn ?
          board.playerOneColor : board.playerTwoColor);
      }
    ]]>
```

```
    </fx:Script>
    <s:layout>
      <s:BasicLayout/>
    </s:layout>
    <s:Panel title="Only connect!" x="10" y="10">
      <s:layout>
        <s:VerticalLayout paddingLeft="5" paddingTop="5"
          paddingBottom="5" paddingRight="5"/>
      </s:layout>
      <s:HGroup verticalAlign="middle">
        <s:Button label="New Game" click="board.newGame()"/>
        <s:Ellipse width="20" height="20"
          fill="{getColor(board.playerOneTurn)}"/>
        <s:Label
          text="Player {board.playerOneTurn ? 1' : '2'} Turn"/>
      </s:HGroup>
      <comp:BoardDisplay id="board"/>
    </s:Panel>
</s:Application>
```

❶ The New Game button calls the newGame function of our BoardDisplay.

❷ We show a little Ellipse filled with the color of the player (player 1 is red; player 2 is black).

❸ We indicate whose turn it is with a Label whose text contains a binding to the playerOneTurn flag. Once again, we see how data binding makes creating UIs simple—and how it makes XML seem even terse.

❹ We create our BoardDisplay component.

Next, we create the BoardDisplay component. We start by doing a copy-paste-modify of the OnlyConnectBoard.fxg document that was saved from Illustrator, and then we add the ActionScript code for the game logic. We also add data bindings into the FXG code. There's a lot of code, so we'll split the explanation into two parts.

session14/session14a/src/components/BoardDisplay.mxml

```
<?xml version="1.0" encoding="utf-8"?>
<Graphic version="1.0" viewHeight="601" viewWidth="701"
  xmlns="library://ns.adobe.com/flex/spark"
  xmlns:fx="http://ns.adobe.com/mxml/2009"
```

```
      xmlns:mx="library://ns.adobe.com/flex/halo"
      click="clickHandler(event)">
<fx:Script><![CDATA[
    import mx.controls.Alert;

    [Bindable]
    public var playerOneColor:uint = 0xFF0000;                    ← ❶

    [Bindable]
    public var playerTwoColor:uint = 0x000000;

    private static const EMPTY_COLOR:uint = 0xFFFFFF;             ← ❷

    [Bindable]
    private var _boardData:Array;                                ← ❸

    [Bindable]
    public var playerOneTurn:Boolean = true;                     ← ❹

    private static const P1:int = 1;                             ← ❺
    private static const P2:int = 2;
    private static const NONE:int = 0;

    public function newGame():void {
      playerOneTurn = true;
      var boardData:Array = new Array();
      for (var row:int = 0; row < 6; row++) {                    ❻
        boardData[row] = [NONE, NONE, NONE, NONE, NONE, NONE, NONE]; ←
      }
      _boardData = boardData;
    }
                                                                 ❼
    private function getColor(row:int, col:int, board:Array):uint { ←
      switch (_boardData[row][col]) {
        case P1:
          return playerOneColor;
        case P2:
          return playerTwoColor;
        default:
          return EMPTY_COLOR;
      }
    }

    private function clickHandler(event:MouseEvent):void {       ← ❽
      var column:int = (event.localX - 5) / 100;
```

```
    var row:int = getDropRow(column);
    if (row == -1) {
      Alert.show("The column is full.", "Illegal Move");
    } else {
      _boardData[row][column] = playerOneTurn ? P1 : P2;      ⬅——— 9
      playerOneTurn = !playerOneTurn;
      _boardData = _boardData.slice(0);                        ⬅┐
    }                                                           10
  }

  private function getDropRow(column:int):int {               ⬅┐
    for (var i:int = 5; i >= 0; i--) {                         11
      if (_boardData[i][column] == NONE) {
        return i;
      }
    }
    return -1;
  }
]]></fx:Script>
...
```

❶ The playerOneColor (red) and playerTwoColor (black) are variables, in case you want to make them settable by the user later.

❷ The EMPTY_COLOR (white) is used to fill spots where there's no game piece.

❸ The _boardData is a simple, two-dimensional Array, which is an Array of Arrays. (I'm trying to keep this example small, so I'm not building a full object model.)

❹ This contains a Boolean flag for whose turn it is: player 1 or player 2.

❺ These are the constants for whether a board position has a player 1 piece (P1), a player 2 piece (P2), or no piece (NONE).

❻ We initialize each row to an Array of NONE ints for the columns. Note that the outer Arrays are the rows and the inner Arrays are the columns.

❼ This function returns the color of a given board position based on the _boardData for that row and column.

❽ We handle clicks on the board. The columns go from 5 to 105, 106 to 205, and so on. Therefore, subtracting 5 and then using an integer division gets the column. We then call getDropRow() to determine the row to insert the player's piece in, and display an alert message if every row is full.

❾ We assign either `P1` or `P2` to the given location in the `_boardData[row][column]` based on whose turn it is.

❿ To refresh the bindings in the game board, we assign the `_boardData` to a copy of itself. This is a very inefficient hack, which will get refactored away later in this workshop session.

⓫ The `getDropRow` function finds the lowest row (i.e., with the highest index, based on how we constructed the 2D `Array`) with a `NONE` value in that column.

Continuing along, let's see the game board.

session14/session14a/src/components/BoardDisplay.mxml (continued)

```
...
  <Group>
    <Rect x="0" y="0" width="700" height="600">
      <fill>
        <SolidColor color="#8E6B23"/>                                    ◁─┐
      </fill>                                                              ❶
      <stroke>
        <SolidColorStroke caps="none" weight="1"
joints="miter" miterLimit="4"/>
      </stroke>
    </Rect>
    <Ellipse x="5" y="4" width="90" height="90">
      <fill>                                                             ❷
        <SolidColor color="{getColor(0, 0, _boardData)}"/>             ◁─┘
      </fill>
      <stroke>
        <SolidColorStroke caps="none" weight="1"
joints="miter" miterLimit="4"/>
      </stroke>
    </Ellipse>
    <Ellipse x="5" y="104" width="90" height="90">
      <fill>
        <SolidColor color="{getColor(1, 0, _boardData)}"/>
      </fill>
      <stroke>
        <SolidColorStroke caps="none" weight="1"
joints="miter" miterLimit="4"/>
      </stroke>
```

```
      </Ellipse>
…a bunch of Ellipses with bindings pasted in…
    <Ellipse x="605" y="505" width="90" height="90">
      <fill>
        <SolidColor color="{getColor(5, 6, _boardData)}"/>
      </fill>
      <stroke>
        <SolidColorStroke caps="none" weight="1"
joints="miter" miterLimit="4"/>
      </stroke>
    </Ellipse>
  </Group>
</Graphic>
```

❶ The Rect of the game board has a fill we set ourselves, instead of in Illustrator.

❷ The Ellipse elements all have their fill set by data bindings.

COLOR IS NOT KIND TO SOME PEOPLE.

HEY!

This is essentially identical to the FXG produced by Illustrator, except that I've set a fill on the Rect to give it a nice background color and set the fill of the Ellipses based on data bindings. Note how each of the data bindings passes in the row and column that the Ellipse corresponds to in the _boardData, and it passes the _boardData in as well. Since we include the _boardData itself in the binding, then the binding will be triggered when we assign the _boardData variable.

This is a "big hammer" approach, which clobbers the entire Array by assigning a temporary variable. Yes, this means that every time a move happens, every square on the whole game board is redrawn! Obviously, this isn't very efficient and is coupled with a hackish way of using data binding.

But the point here isn't that our code is going to win an efficiency contest: *it's that we drew all the MXML in Illustrator.* If you've ever worked with designers, you know that staying true to the visual design is crucial—and that what may seem unimportant to a programmer is essential to a designer. So, FXG helps us bridge that gap, which is awesome.

Running the app, we see the screens we showed earlier.

Next, we're going to do two refactorings. First, we'll refactor the app to create the board programmatically, instead of using the FXG that we got from Illustrator. Since an Only Connect board is a simple pattern, this will be easy to do. We'll also fix the code so that redrawing every Ellipse when a move is made won't be required. Then, we'll factor out the board data into its own class and add victory condition checking logic.

So, let's start with the first refactoring. We begin by making a small change to the main app.

session14/session14b/src/OnlyConnect.mxml

```
...
    import mx.graphics.SolidColor;

    private function getColor(playerOneTurn:Boolean):SolidColor {
      return new SolidColor(playerOneTurn ?
        board.playerOneColor : board.playerTwoColor);
      return playerOneTurn ?
        board.playerOneFill : board.playerTwoFill;              ❶
    }
...
```

❶ Instead of having the board return the colors of player 1 and 2, it's returning the fills they now use. This is better since we don't need to create a new SolidColor here every time.

Now, let's move on to the BoardDisplay. It has changed enough that it's easiest to show it as a new file rather than showing the differences. So, here's the refactored code:

session14/session14b/src/BoardDisplay.mxml

```
<?xml version="1.0" encoding="utf-8"?>
<Graphic version="1.0" viewHeight="601" viewWidth="701"
  xmlns="library://ns.adobe.com/flex/spark"
  xmlns:fx="http://ns.adobe.com/mxml/2009"
  xmlns:mx="library://ns.adobe.com/flex/halo"
  initialize="createBoard()"                                   ❶
  click="clickHandler(event)">
<fx:Script><![CDATA[
  import mx.controls.Alert;
```

```
import spark.primitives.Rect;
import mx.graphics.SolidColorStroke;
import mx.graphics.SolidColor;
import spark.primitives.Ellipse;

[Bindable]
public var playerOneFill:SolidColor = new SolidColor(0xFF0000);   ←── ②

[Bindable]
public var playerTwoFill:SolidColor = new SolidColor(0x000000);

private static const EMPTY_FILL:SolidColor =
  new SolidColor(0xFFFFFF);

[Bindable]
private var _boardData:Array;

[Bindable]
private var _board:Array;                          ←──── ③

[Bindable]
public var playerOneTurn:Boolean = true;

private static const P1:int = 1;
private static const P2:int = 2;
private static const NONE:int = 0;

public function newGame():void {
  playerOneTurn = true;                            ④
  _boardData = new Array();                    ←──┘
  for (var row:int = 0; row < 6; row++) {
    _boardData[row] = [NONE, NONE, NONE, NONE, NONE, NONE, NONE];
  }
  if (_board != null) updateBoard();            ←──┐
}                                                   ⑤

private function createBoard():void {            ←──
  newGame();                                        ⑥
  _board = new Array(6);
  for (var row:int = 0; row < 6; row++) {
    _board[row] = new Array(7);
    for (var col:int = 0; col < 7; col++) {
      _board[row][col] = addEllipse(row, col);
    }
  }
}
```

```
private function updateBoard():void {                         ⑦
  for (var row:int = 0; row < 6; row++) {
    for (var col:int = 0; col < 7; col++) {
      Ellipse(_board[row][col]).fill = getFill(row, col);
    }
  }
}
```

❶ We call createBoard() when the initialize event is broadcast

❷ We switch to specifying a SolidColor for player 1 and 2 and the empty fill, rather than specifying the color uint for each. These are the standard 24-bit RGB hexadecimal color values.

❸ We create a new Array for the board, to store a reference to each Ellipse we create.

❹ Because we are no longer relying on "hackishly" triggering bindings to the _boardData, we no longer need to use a temporary variable when building the board data.

❺ We call updateBoard() once the board is initialized. Yes, we could have just done this inside the newGame loop, but that would be making that function do too much. This way, if we implement loading, the updateBoard function can be reused to update the board based on the state of the _boardData.

❻ The createBoard function calls newGame to create the boardData (which won't trigger updateBoard since there's no _board yet) and then creates the _board by calling addEllipse() for each row and column. (If you're thinking that it's unseemly having so much model code in the BoardDisplay, I agree with you—that's the subject of the next refactoring.)

❼ The updateBoard function updates the fills of the Ellipses based on the calling getFill. This only needs to be called on newGame or (hypothetically) when loading; there's a much more efficient way of handling this at the end of a turn.

Continuing along, here's the rest of the file:

```
…continued from earlier…
  private function getFill(row:int, col:int):SolidColor {
    switch (_boardData[row][col]) {
```

```
        case P1:
          return playerOneFill;
        case P2:
          return playerTwoFill;
        default:
          return EMPTY_FILL;
    }
}

private function clickHandler(event:MouseEvent):void {
  var column:int = (event.localX - 5) / 100;
  var row:int = getDropRow(column);
  if (row == -1) {
    Alert.show("The column is full.", "Illegal Move");
  } else {
    _boardData[row][column] = playerOneTurn ? P1 : P2;
    Ellipse(_board[row][column]).fill = getFill(row, column);     ◁────
    var winner:int = checkWinner();                                      ❽
    if (winner != NONE) {
      Alert.show("Player " + (winner == P1 ? "1" : "2") + " wins",◁┐
        "Victory!");                                                    ❾
    }
    playerOneTurn = !playerOneTurn;
  }
}

private function getDropRow(column:int):int {
  for (var i:int = 5; i >= 0; i--) {
    if (_boardData[i][column] == NONE) {
      return i;
    }
  }
  return -1;
}

private function addEllipse(row:int, col:int):Ellipse {    ◁────
  var ellipse:Ellipse = new Ellipse();                            ❿
  ellipse.x = 4 + col*100;
  ellipse.y = 5 + row*100;
  ellipse.width = 90;
  ellipse.height = 90;
  ellipse.fill = getFill(row,col);
  ellipse.stroke = new SolidColorStroke(0x000000, 1, 1.0, false,
    "normal", null, "miter", 4);
```

```
    boardGroup.addElement(ellipse);
    return ellipse;
  }

  private function checkWinner():int {                    ⟵
    return NONE;
  }                                                        ⓫

]]></fx:Script>
  <Group id="boardGroup">
    <Rect x="0" y="0" width="700" height="600">
      <fill>
        <SolidColor color="#8E6B23"/>
      </fill>
      <stroke>
        <SolidColorStroke caps="none" weight="1"/>
      </stroke>
    </Rect>                                                ⓬
  </Group>                                                ⟵
</Graphic>
```

❽   When a move is made, we only set the fill of the Ellipse at the _board[row][column].

❾   We call a checkWinner() function, and if the winner isn't NONE we show an alert message.

❿   The addEllipse function creates the board the same way that it was done in the FXG produced by Illustrator. (If you run this app, you'll be hard-pressed to tell the difference.)

⓫   This function is stubbed out. If you want to practice your Action-Script 3 skills, implement it before reading the next file.

⓬   Note how there is nothing more inside the Group than just the Rect now. All the Ellipses are created by addEllipse.

That's it!

Running the app, we see no real change from before, which is always the goal when refactoring.

Before moving on to the next workshop session, let's think about what we've done. We've created a BoardDisplay that has a bunch of game logic muddled together with display logic. So, let's refactor it again and create a Board model class to handle the game logic. Also, while we're at it, let's implement the checkWinner function. Note that the way that I'm going to implement checkWinner will be pretty inefficient; I'm trying to keep the code somewhat readable. I'm not even going to use the recent move to limit what the function is checking; instead, I'm just going to search the entire board for a winner. (Exercise for the reader: refactor my code!)

Let's start by creating the Board class, and then refactor the BoardDisplay class to use it.

session14/session14c/src/Board.as

```
package model {
  public class Board {
    public static const P1:int = 1;
    public static const P2:int = 2;
    public static const NONE:int = 0;

    [Bindable]
    private var _data:Array;                              ◁——————❶

    [Bindable]
    public var playerOneTurn:Boolean = true;

    public function Board() {
    }

    public function newGame():void {                     ◁——————❷
      playerOneTurn = true;
      _data = new Array();
      for (var row:int = 0; row < 6; row++) {
        _data[row] = [NONE, NONE, NONE, NONE, NONE, NONE, NONE];
      }
    }

    public function getData(row:int, col:int):int {      ◁——————❸
      return _data[row][col];
    }

    public function playerMove(column:int):int {         ◁——————❹
      var row:int = getDropRow(column);
      if (row != -1) {
```

```
      _data[row][column] = playerOneTurn ? P1 : P2;
      playerOneTurn = !playerOneTurn;
    }
    return row;
  }

  private function getDropRow(column:int):int {
    for (var i:int = 5; i >= 0; i--) {
      if (_data[i][column] == NONE) {
        return i;
      }
    }
    return -1;
  }
...
```

① The board data is encapsulated in the private _data Array.

② The public newGame function just creates the _data. Also, note that the empty Board() constructor is redundant, since it's what would have been generated by the compiler. However, I have a habit of writing constructors…

③ The public getData function returns the data at the row and column without exposing implementation details.

④ The playerMove function takes the column the player is placing in and returns the row that the player's piece ended up on (or −1 if illegal). If there was a proper object model I wouldn't use −1, but there isn't.

Continuing along, here's the rest of the file. Note that I'm omitting the implementations of some of the victory checking functions, since there's nothing particularly exciting in them. However, if you are new to ActionScript 3 you may enjoy writing your own victory checking algorithm and/or downloading the code zip file from the book's website and reading through mine to see how you can improve it. The row and column victory checking is easy, but the diagonal victory checking is a bit more annoying to get right. Furthermore, if you care about efficiency you could take the last move into account to reduce the number of tests that the code does.

```
…continued from earlier…
    public function checkWinner():int {                              ◄———— ❺
      var rowWinner:int = getRowWinner();
      if (rowWinner != NONE) return rowWinner;
      var columnWinner:int = getColumnWinner();
      if (columnWinner != NONE) return columnWinner;
      var forwardDiagWinner:int = getForwardDiagWinner();
      if (forwardDiagWinner != NONE) return forwardDiagWinner;
      return getBackwardDiagWinner();
    }

    private function getRowWinner():int {                            ◄———— ❻
      var lenP1:int = 0;
      var lenP2:int = 0;
      for (var row:int = 0; row < 6; row++) {
        lenP1 = _data[row][0] == P1 ? 1 : 0;
        lenP2 = _data[row][0] == P2 ? 1 : 0;
        for (var col:int = 1; col < 7; col++) {
          if (_data[row][col] == P1) {
            lenP2 = 0;
            if (_data[row][col-1] == P1) {
              lenP1++;
              if (lenP1 > 3) return P1;
            } else {
              lenP1 = 1;
            }
          } else if (_data[row][col] == P2) {
            lenP1 = 0;
            if (_data[row][col-1] == P2) {
              lenP2++;
              if (lenP2 > 3) return P2;
            } else {
              lenP2 = 1;
            }
          } else {
            lenP2 = 0;
            lenP1 = 0;
          }
        }
      }
      return NONE;
    }
```

EVEN *I* COULD WRITE BETTER CODE THAN THIS!

NOW *THATS* LOW

```
    private function getColumnWinner():int {                    ← ❼
...a bunch of tedious code (see the code zip file)…
    }

    private function getForwardDiagWinner():int {              ← ❽
...a bunch of tedious code (see the code zip file)…
    }

    private function getBackwardDiagWinner():int {             ← ❾
...a bunch of tedious code (see the code zip file)…
  }
}
```

❺ The `checkWinner` function checks whether there are four of the same player's pieces in a row in any row, column, or diagonal by calling functions that do the messy work.

❻ The `getRowWinner` function checks a row for four in a row.

❼ The `getColumnWinner` function checks a column for four in a row.

❽ The `getForwardDiagWinner` function checks a forward-leaning diagonal for four in a row.

❾ The `getBackwardDiagWinner` function checks a backward-leaning diagonal for four in a row.

Now that we have created the `Board` class, we can refactor the `BoardDisplay` to use it. Again, the `BoardDisplay` will change enough that it's easiest to show it as a new file. Also, as a bonus for reading this far, I'm going to throw in a gratuitous 3D effect as a preview of some of the fun we'll have in the next chapter.

session14/session14c/src/BoardDisplay.mxml

```
<?xml version="1.0" encoding="utf-8"?>
<Graphic version="1.0" viewHeight="601" viewWidth="701"
  xmlns="library://ns.adobe.com/flex/spark"
  xmlns:fx="http://ns.adobe.com/mxml/2009"
  xmlns:mx="library://ns.adobe.com/flex/halo"
  initialize="createBoard()"
  click="clickHandler(event)">
<fx:Script><![CDATA[
```

```
import model.Board;
import mx.controls.Alert;
import spark.primitives.Rect;
import mx.graphics.SolidColorStroke;
import mx.graphics.SolidColor;
import spark.primitives.Ellipse;

[Bindable]
public var playerOneFill:SolidColor = new SolidColor(0xFF0000);

[Bindable]
public var playerTwoFill:SolidColor = new SolidColor(0x000000);

private static const EMPTY_FILL:SolidColor =
  new SolidColor(0xFFFFFF);

[Bindable]
private var _board:Board;                                    ① ◁──┐

[Bindable]
private var _ellipses:Array;

public function newGame():void {
  _board.newGame();
  updateBoard();
}

public function get playerOneTurn():Boolean {
  return _board.playerOneTurn;
}

private function createBoard():void {
  _board = new Board();                          ◁──────────── ②
  _board.newGame();
  _ellipses = new Array(6);
  for (var row:int = 0; row < 6; row++) {
    _ellipses[row] = new Array(7);
    for (var col:int = 0; col < 7; col++) {
      _ellipses[row][col] = addEllipse(row, col);
    }
  }
}
```

```
private function updateBoard():void {
  for (var row:int = 0; row < 6; row++) {
    for (var col:int = 0; col < 7; col++) {
      Ellipse(_ellipses[row][col]).fill = getFill(row, col);
    }
  }
  newGameEffect.play();                                    ◁——— ❸
}
...
```

❶ The _board variable is the new Board type.

❷ We create a new Board in createBoard, and we don't need any cheesy null checking anymore.

❸ When the board is updated (on a new game or the hypothetical load game), we play our new effect.

Continuing along, here's the rest of the file.

```
...continued from earlier...
  private function getFill(row:int, col:int):SolidColor {
    switch (_board.getData(row, col)) {
      case Board.P1:                                       ◁——— ❹
        return playerOneFill;
      case Board.P2:
        return playerTwoFill;
      default:
        return EMPTY_FILL;
    }
  }

  private function clickHandler(event:MouseEvent):void {
    var column:int = (event.localX - 5) / 100;
    var row:int = _board.playerMove(column);
    if (row != -1) {
      Ellipse(_ellipses[row][column]).fill = getFill(row, column);
      var winner:int = _board.checkWinner();              ◁—┐
      if (winner != Board.NONE) {                            ❺
        Alert.show(
          "Player " + (winner == Board.P1 ? "1" : "2") + " wins",
          "Victory!");
      }
    } else {
```

```
        Alert.show("The column is full.", "Illegal Move");
      }
    }

  private function addEllipse(row:int, col:int):Ellipse {
    var ellipse:Ellipse = new Ellipse();
    ellipse.x = 4 + col*100;
    ellipse.y = 5 + row*100;
    ellipse.width = 90;
    ellipse.height = 90;
    ellipse.fill = getFill(row,col);
    ellipse.stroke = new SolidColorStroke(0x000000, 1, 1.0, false,
      "normal", null, "miter", 4);
    boardGroup.addElement(ellipse);
    return ellipse;
  }
]]></fx:Script>
<fx:Declarations>                                               ❻
  <Rotate3D duration="1000" id="newGameEffect"
    angleXFrom="0" angleXTo="360" target="{this}"/>
</fx:Declarations>
  <Group id="boardGroup">
    <Rect x="0" y="0" width="700" height="600">
      <fill>
        <SolidColor color="#8E6B23"/>
      </fill>
      <stroke>
        <SolidColorStroke caps="none" weight="1"/>
      </stroke>
    </Rect>
  </Group>
</Graphic>
```

❹ The `getData` function of the `Board` is now called, and the P1 and P2 constants now belong to the `Board`.

❺ The `Board`'s `checkWinner` function is called.

❻ Inside the declarations, we create a new `Rotate3D` effect. Effects will be explained in the next chapter. Note how the `fill` child element of the `Rect` is assigning the `SolidColor` to the `fill` property of the `Rect`. It's not magic, it's property assignment. This is why the same namespace (in this case, the default namespace) is used.

That's it! Run the application; you'll see the same app as before but with the new Rotate3D effect, shown here. Also, you can play a game and test the victory condition checking.

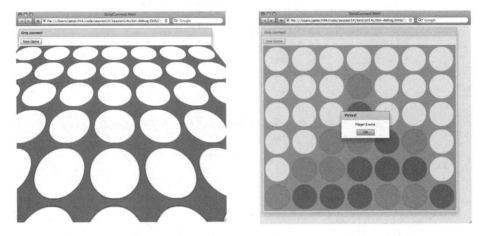

Not only has this been your first taste of a larger Flex 4 application, but you've also seen how refactoring Flex code works. We started with generated FXG code, added some business logic, replaced the repetitive FXG with programmatically generated graphics, and then factored out the business logic into its own class. In the real world, you'd build a proper object model, not just a Board class and ints. Furthermore, in chapter 7 we'll see how an even larger Flex application is structured using the Cairngorm framework.

The impressive thing is that all this started with a drawing in Illustrator that could have been done by your designer, and he or she would probably feel that you stayed close enough to the design in the finished output. Note that Flash Catalyst makes this designer-developer workflow even better, but that topic is beyond the scope of this book.

Key points

- FXG produced by tools such as Illustrator or Photoshop can be a good starting point for Flex code.
- As a developer, you probably want to look at places you can refactor once you have confidence in the design. You can also generate graphics using the Spark primitives we saw in session 11.
- Business logic belongs in model classes, not mixed in with view code.

SESSION 15 Camera and video—a fake Twitter client

Well, this chapter started innocently enough, but that last workshop session sure had a lot of code in it, didn't it? In this workshop session, the last in the chapter, we'll have a little bit of fun building a toy example that fits on just over half a page of code. And what's more fun than playing with a video camera? In the process, you'll learn how to use the Flash `Camera` and `Video` classes with Flex applications, since the API docs for these classes are focused on doing this using just plain Action-Script 3, not a Flex app. Since I had to scratch my head a bit to figure this out, I hope I'll save you from having to do the same.

So, hopefully your computer has a camera built in (thanks, Apple!) or attached to it. What we're going to build is an app that looks like this:

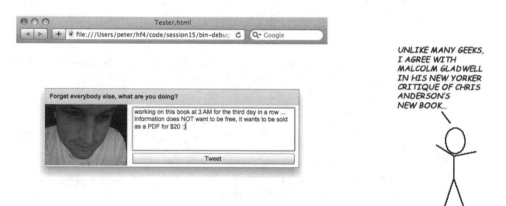

UNLIKE MANY GEEKS, I AGREE WITH MALCOLM GLADWELL IN HIS NEW YORKER CRITIQUE OF CHRIS ANDERSON'S NEW BOOK...

This is a totally fake Twitter client, and that's me, really tired, captured by my laptop camera. Why a fake Twitter client? Well, this book, like the rest of the tech community, is obsessed with Twitter—so why not? More seriously, the idea is that the Twitter client would take a picture of you when you tweeted, and then post that picture to Flickr. It would then create a shortened URL of that picture (using bit.ly presumably) and insert that URL in your tweet (if there was room). So then, your countless followers could see what you were doing (or how tired you were looking) at the time you were tweeting. (And then they could reply to you telling you to stop tweeting and go to bed.)

We'll build a real Twitter client in chapter 7. Taking that code and adapting it to do the what I just described is an exercise for the reader.

Without further ado, let's see the code.

Session15/src/Tester.mxml

```
<?xml version="1.0" encoding="utf-8"?>
<s:Application
  xmlns:fx="http://ns.adobe.com/mxml/2009"
  xmlns:s="library://ns.adobe.com/flex/spark"
  xmlns:mx="library://ns.adobe.com/flex/halo"
  width="100%" height="100%"
  applicationComplete="onApplicationComplete(event)">
<fx:Script><![CDATA[
  import mx.controls.Alert;
  import mx.events.FlexEvent;
  import flash.media.Camera;
  import flash.media.Video;

  private function onApplicationComplete(event:FlexEvent):void {
    var camera:Camera = Camera.getCamera();           <--  1
    if (camera == null) {
      Alert.show("Buy a Mac.", "No Camera!");
      return;                                               2
    }
    var video:Video = new Video(160,120);              <--
    video.attachCamera(camera);                      <--  3
    videoHolder.addChild(video);                     <--  4
    focusManager.setFocus(tweetTA);                  <--
  }                                                        5
]]></fx:Script>
  <s:Panel x="{width/2 - 250}" y="{height/2 - 80}"
    width="500" height="155"
    title="Forget everybody else, what are you doing?">    6
    <s:SpriteVisualElement id="videoHolder" width="100%"  <--
      height="100%"/>
    <s:TextArea id="tweetTA" x="170" y="5" width="320"     <--
      height="85" maxChars="140"/>
    <s:Button label="Tweet" x="170" y="95" width="320"/>   7
  </s:Panel>
</s:Application>
```

1. Get the Camera.
2. Create a new Video object to show video.
3. Attach the Camera to the Video object.
4. Add the Video object to the SpriteVisualElement, which can have Sprites added to it.
5. Automatically focus the TextArea, since you are supposed to be tweeting and not just looking at yourself.
6. Create a new SpriteVisualElement.
7. Create a new TextArea for your tweet.

Save the application and run it; you'll probably see an Adobe Flash Player Settings security dialog first (shown here). Click Allow to allow camera access.

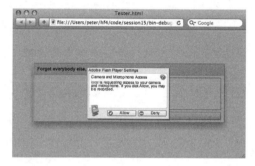

If you still see no video, what you may need to do is change the camera type to USB class video.

Switch to the camera icon tab, choose USB Video Class Video, and click Close.

That's it!

➤ Key points

- Flex lets you do cool things like play with the user's camera with very little code.
- The SpriteVisualElement class can have children added to it with addChild.

What's next?

Well, this has been both a whirlwind tour of the Spark components and a deep dive into building and refactoring a real Flex app — starting with an FXG drawing exported from Adobe Illustrator.

In the next chapter you'll learn about Spark containers and layouts, as well as view states, effects, styling and skinning. View states are much improved in Flex 4, so they can be effectively used for navigation and state changes in your apps. This is also fortunate, since there's currently *(as of Flex 4 Beta 2; this may change!)* no Spark equivalent for the Halo navigator containers you'll learn about in chapter 5. So if you want to stay Spark-only in your apps, you need to become a view states master.

Finally, by the end of the next chapter, you'll have a deeper understanding of the Spark component model.

4

Spark containers, view states, effects, and styling

In this chapter, we'll dive deeper into Spark and into Flex 4 in general. You'll learn how to use Spark containers and layouts—we've already seen them throughout the book, but it will be good to spend a bit of time discussing them. Then, we'll talk about view states, which are much improved in Flex 4—and which are much more necessary, since there's no Spark equivalent of the Halo navigator containers, as you'll see in the next chapter. Next we'll explore basic effects and CSS styling, and conclude the chapter by peeking behind the MXML curtain to view the code Flex generates for us and some of the events dispatched in the Spark component lifecycle.

BESIDES, THIS IS THE KIND OF THING THAT YOU WOULD BUILD IN FLASH CATALYST. IT'S BASICALLY THE "HELLO WORLD" OF FLASH CATALYST. SO, WE'RE SKIPPING IT.

Note that in a longer book, each of these topics would have its own 20–30-page chapter. We're going to see what you can absorb in about 30 pages. Because of this, there won't be an example of adding to a Button a custom skin that looks like a pizza, for example. And I'm even not going to show you the now seemingly obligatory "custom ScrollBar with something cheesy (like, say, a pizza) as a thumbIcon" example.

So, let's get started.

SESSION 16 Spark containers and layouts

In this workshop session, you'll learn about the Spark containers and layouts. We've already seen many of these in the book so far (how could we avoid them?), but now we'll cover them properly. Briefly, containers are where we add our UI controls (both Spark and Halo controls and Spark primitives) in our Flex application—essentially, a Flex app is just a bunch of components that live in a variety of containers and that respond to events. We've already discussed events and components; now it's time to focus on containers.

Containers such as Group and its subclasses HGroup and VGroup take as children any components that implement the IUIComponent or IGraphicElement interfaces, so they can contain both Spark components and primitives. Containers that extend SkinnableContainerBase can have children and custom skins.

Let's start by showing the class hierarchy, since we'll be building four examples that use it:

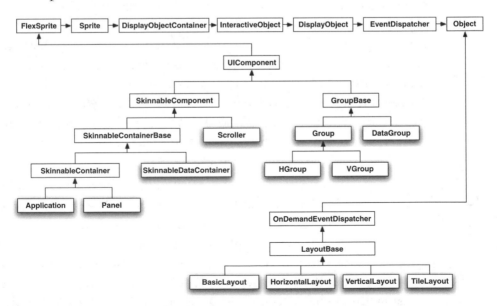

The classes that we'll use in this session have shadows. Briefly, you'll see that Application, Panel, SkinnableDataContainer, and Scroller all extend SkinnableComponent, so they can be skinned. And the BasicLayout, HorizontalLayout, VerticalLayout, and TileLayout all extend LayoutBase for common functionality.

We'll begin by building an app that looks like this, in order to demonstrate the basic use of Group and Layout classes:

session16/session16a/src/Tester.mxml

```xml
<?xml version="1.0" encoding="utf-8"?>
<s:Application
  xmlns:fx="http://ns.adobe.com/mxml/2009"
  xmlns:s="library://ns.adobe.com/flex/spark"
  xmlns:mx="library://ns.adobe.com/flex/halo"
  width="100%" height="100%">
  <s:Group x="10" y="10">
    <s:layout>
      <s:VerticalLayout gap="20"/>              ①
    </s:layout>
    <s:HGroup>
      <s:VGroup>
        <s:Button label="1"/>
        <s:Button label="2"/>
      </s:VGroup>
      <s:Button label="3"/>
      <s:Button label="4"/>
    </s:HGroup>
    <s:Group>
      <s:layout>
        <s:HorizontalLayout paddingLeft="15"/>   ②
      </s:layout>
      <s:Button label="5"/>
      <s:Button label="6"/>
      <s:Button label="7"/>
      <s:Button label="8"/>
    </s:Group>
  </s:Group>
</s:Application>
```

1 The outer `Group` has a `VerticalLayout` and contains an `HGroup` (with `Buttons` 1–4) and a `Group` with a `HorizontalLayout` that contains `Buttons` 5–8.

2 The `Layout` classes can have more attributes set on them than are exposed by the `HGroup` and `VGroup` classes.

Next, we'll look at the `Panel` container, as well as see how to swap layouts at runtime. The app we're going to build looks like the following when launched:

It has a `DropDownList` that lets us choose between `BasicLayout`, `VerticalLayout`, `HorizontalLayout`, and `TileLayout`. As shown by the following screenshots, the Spark `Panel` container doesn't clip its children, unlike the Halo `Panel` container. (This is a performance optimization, since some `Panels` don't need to scroll; as we'll see later this workshop session, adding scrolling is easy.)

Note that switching back to `BasicLayout` leaves the x and y locations unchanged (because it's a no-op layout), so they keep whatever the previous layout did to them. In this case, switching back from a `TileLayout` produces the following result (the way you tell the difference is by looking at the content of the `DropDownList`):

Without further ado, let's see the code that does this. Note that this code is in a new project in the session16 folder.

session16/session16b/src/Tester.mxml

```
<?xml version="1.0" encoding="utf-8"?>
<s:Application
  xmlns:fx="http://ns.adobe.com/mxml/2009"
  xmlns:s="library://ns.adobe.com/flex/spark"
  xmlns:mx="library://ns.adobe.com/flex/halo"
  width="100%" height="100%">
<fx:Script><![CDATA[
  import spark.layouts.BasicLayout;
  import mx.collections.ArrayCollection;
  import spark.layouts.TileLayout;
  import spark.layouts.HorizontalLayout;
  import spark.layouts.VerticalLayout;

  private var _basicLayout:BasicLayout = new BasicLayout();
  private var _verticalLayout:VerticalLayout =
    new VerticalLayout();
  private var _horizontalLayout:HorizontalLayout =
    new HorizontalLayout();
  private var _tileLayout:TileLayout = new TileLayout();

  [Bindable]
  private var _layouts:ArrayCollection = new ArrayCollection([      ←——— ❶
    _basicLayout, _verticalLayout, _horizontalLayout,
    _tileLayout]);
]]></fx:Script>
  <s:Panel x="15" y="15" width="240" height="140">
    <s:layout>
```

```
            <s:VerticalLayout paddingLeft="10" paddingTop="10"/>
          </s:layout>
          <s:DropDownList id="layoutsDDL" dataProvider="{_layouts}"
            width="200" selectedIndex="0"/>
          <s:Group height="50" layout="{layoutsDDL.selectedItem}">
            <s:Button label="a"/>
            <s:Button label="b"/>
            <s:Button label="c"/>
            <s:Button label="d"/>
          </s:Group>
      </s:Panel>
</s:Application>
```

❷

❶ We create a new `ArrayCollection` of the various layout objects we want to explore, and store it in `_layouts`, which is assigned to the `dataProvider` of the `layoutsDDL` DropDownList. Briefly, layout objects such as `VerticalLayout` and `HorizontalLayout` define how the children of their container are arranged—by specifying one, you are essentially providing an algorithm, neatly packaged as an object.

❷ We bind the `selectedItem` of the `layoutsDDL` to the `layout` property of the `Group` that contains the four buttons. That way, when the user picks another layout from the drop-down list, the binding will trigger, and the chosen layout object will be set as the layout for the group.

Unlike in Halo, where the layout was fairly tightly coupled to the code for the container, in Spark the layout is completely decoupled from the container. (Extremely advanced developers could subvert the layout done by Halo containers, but this remained beyond the reach of us mere mortals, for whom a VBox lays out its children vertically, period.) This means you can write your own layout classes, which you can use instead of the built-in ones. (If you think that frameworks like Flex are all about inheritance and huge class hierarchies, this fact shows how composition plays an important role in more flexible ones.) These layouts can be used statically or they can be dynamically swapped in, as in the previous example. Andrew Trice wrote a good article at InsideRIA (www.insideria.com/2009/05/flex-4-custom-layouts.html) that explains how to build a custom layout class, so take a look if you're interested.

Next, let's see what happens when we add a `Scroller` to the mix. A `Scroller` shows a scrollable component and horizontal and vertical scrollbars. The scrollable component is called a viewport, and it must implement the `IViewport` interface. We'll also change the height to not be fixed at 50, since we want the content to be able to grow to trigger the vertical scrolling. Of course, this will change the behavior of our `TileLayout`.

These screenshots show the behavior of the app we are about to build. It's similar to the app we just built, but I'm showing all the code so you can follow along without reading "diff"-style code listings. Note how the `TileLayout` uses only one column when its height isn't constrained.

Let's see the code; note that this is in a new project in the session16 folder.

session16/session16c/src/Tester.mxml

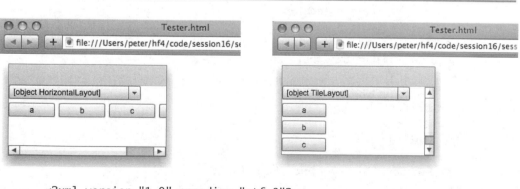

```
<?xml version="1.0" encoding="utf-8"?>
<s:Application
```

```
        xmlns:fx="http://ns.adobe.com/mxml/2009"
        xmlns:s="library://ns.adobe.com/flex/spark"
        xmlns:mx="library://ns.adobe.com/flex/halo"
        width="100%" height="100%">
<fx:Script><![CDATA[
    import spark.layouts.BasicLayout;
    import mx.collections.ArrayCollection;
    import spark.layouts.TileLayout;
    import spark.layouts.HorizontalLayout;
    import spark.layouts.VerticalLayout;

    private var _basicLayout:BasicLayout = new BasicLayout();
    private var _verticalLayout:VerticalLayout =
        new VerticalLayout();
    private var _horizontalLayout:HorizontalLayout =
        new HorizontalLayout();
    private var _tileLayout:TileLayout = new TileLayout();

    [Bindable]
    private var _layouts:ArrayCollection = new ArrayCollection([
        _basicLayout, _verticalLayout, _horizontalLayout,
        _tileLayout]);
]]></fx:Script>
    <s:Panel x="15" y="15" width="240" height="140">                    ❶
        <s:Scroller width="100%" height="100%">
            <s:VGroup>                                                 ❷
                <s:DropDownList id="layoutsDDL"
                    dataProvider="{_layouts}"
                    width="200" selectedIndex="0"/>
                <s:Group layout="{layoutsDDL.selectedItem}">
                    <s:Button label="a"/>
                    <s:Button label="b"/>
                    <s:Button label="c"/>
                    <s:Button label="d"/>
                </s:Group>
            </s:VGroup>
        </s:Scroller>
    </s:Panel>
</s:Application>
```

❶ The Scroller is a child of the Panel class.

❷ The VGroup inside the Scroller doesn't have a height now, so it can grow to the preferred size of all its children. This lets the VGroup become taller than the area inside the "viewport" of the Scroller, thus triggering the appearance of the ScrollBar.

Finally, let's switch gears and look at DataGroup and SkinnableDataContainer, which are Spark containers with an interesting twist: they can have dataProvider properties that can take primitives and/or components. (Yes, you can even include both at the same time; I'm not sure that you'll ever need to do this, but there's an example in the API docs[1] that shows how to define a DataGroup with a mixture of data and graphical items as its dataProvider.) We'll build an app that shows how to use this dataProvider. While we're at it, we'll also show an example of using SkinnableContainer directly. You won't need to do this unless you're building your own highly customized container (with custom skins from, say, Flash Catalyst), but I want to show it so you know it's there.

The app we're building looks like this:

Let's see the code.

session16/session16d/src/Tester.mxml

```xml
<?xml version="1.0" encoding="utf-8"?>
<s:Application
  xmlns:fx="http://ns.adobe.com/mxml/2009"
  xmlns:s="library://ns.adobe.com/flex/spark"
  xmlns:mx="library://ns.adobe.com/flex/halo"
  width="100%" height="100%">
<fx:Script><![CDATA[
  import mx.collections.ArrayCollection;

  [Bindable]
  private var _fish:ArrayCollection = new ArrayCollection([
    "Halibut", "Salmon", "Tuna"]);
```

❶

[1] http://livedocs.adobe.com/flex/gumbo/langref/spark/components/DataGroup.html#includeExamples-Summary

```
]]></fx:Script>
  <s:layout>
    <s:HorizontalLayout paddingTop="15" paddingLeft="15"/>
  </s:layout>
  <s:SkinnableContainer>
    <s:Button label="a"/>
    <s:Button label="b"/>
  </s:SkinnableContainer>
  <s:SkinnableDataContainer dataProvider="{_fish}"
    itemRenderer="spark.skins.spark.DefaultItemRenderer"/>
  <s:DataGroup dataProvider="{_fish}"
    itemRenderer="spark.skins.spark.DefaultItemRenderer">
    <s:layout>
      <s:HorizontalLayout/>
    </s:layout>
  </s:DataGroup>
</s:Application>
```

❶ We create an ArrayCollection of fish for testing.

❷ This SkinnableContainer by default has a vertical layout. Also, by default it doesn't look any different than a Group—but you could change that.

❸ The SkinnableDataContainer has a VerticalLayout by default.

❹ The DataGroup has a BasicLayout by default, so we give it a HorizontalLayout instead.

So, what's the difference between SkinnableDataContainer and DataGroup? After all, in this example both the SkinnableDataContainer and the DataGroup took a DefaultItemRenderer as their itemRenderer. Sure, we gave the DataGroup a HorizontalLayout, but we could have done that with the SkinnableDataContainer as well.

This is actually one of the points: the default behavior of the SkinnableDataContainer and DataGroup is very similar. However, the difference is that the SkinnableDataContainer is a descendant of SkinnableComponent (via SkinnableContainerBase) and thus is skinnable (hence the name), whereas DataGroup is not. What this means is that the SkinnableDataContainer can have a custom skinClass associated with it to customize its look. (To see how to do this, see the documentation for SkinnableComponent. Also, note that this is a job best done in Flash Catalyst, so I don't want to show it here.) You may recall from the previous chapter that `List` is a descendant of `SkinnableDataContainer` (via `ListBase`). So, now you see where it gets some of its behavior.

We've seen how layouts and containers are separate from each other, so the layouts can be swapped in to the different types of containers with predictable effects. Hooray for composition!

➤ Key points

- ⚙ Layouts and containers are decoupled in Spark, meaning you can write your own layouts to be used with any Spark container.
- ⚙ `DataGroup` and `SkinnableDataContainer` have a `dataProvider` property you can set.

SESSION 17 View states

Now that you know how to use containers to store the components that we're using to build our Flex applications, let's see how to make our Flex applications more dynamic by using view states. In Halo, there are "navigator containers" (which we'll discuss in the next chapter) that let you accomplish this, but if you want to use the Spark approach as much as possible, you'll use view states to build navigation into your Flex apps. View states allow you to change what your application or components look like in response to what state they're in.

FINITE STATE MACHINES? WE CALLED THEM DISCRETE FINITE AUTOMATA IN MY DAY... YOU KIDS DON'T LEARN ANYTHING THESE DAYS WITH YOUR TWITTER AND ADHD...

NOTE FOR THE CS GEEKS

If you're a computer science geek like myself, you'll appreciate that they're called states, since the different view states of a component can be thought of as a finite state machine, with the component being in only one at a time.

In this workshop session, we'll build an app that shows the power of view states, which have a highly improved syntax in Flex 4. In its default state, the app looks like this:

We'll create a custom subclass of `Panel` called `HPanel` (H is for Header, not Horizontal—yes, this is a somewhat awkward name) that adds easy detection of whether its header has been clicked. When any of the `HPanel` headers are clicked, they dispatch an event named `headerClick`. The app then changes state to show just that `HPanel`, as shown in the following three figures. (Note also that we're using Japanese Kanji and resizing the fonts accordingly—primarily to show off how awesome the font support is in Flash 10!)

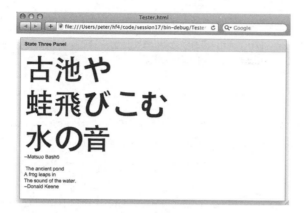

NOW THAT'S MORE LIKE IT. REMINDS ME OF THE GOOD OLD DAYS. HYPERCARD FTW!

Let's see the code, first for the HPanel.

session17/src/components/HPanel.mxml

```xml
<?xml version="1.0" encoding="utf-8"?>
<s:Panel xmlns:fx="http://ns.adobe.com/mxml/2009"
  xmlns:s="library://ns.adobe.com/flex/spark"
  xmlns:mx="library://ns.adobe.com/flex/halo"
  creationComplete="onCreationComplete()">
<fx:Metadata>
  [Event(name="headerClick")]
</fx:Metadata>
<fx:Script><![CDATA[
  import flash.events.Event;
  import spark.skins.spark.PanelSkin;

  private function onCreationComplete():void {
    var panelSkin:PanelSkin = skin as PanelSkin;
    if (panelSkin == null) return;
    panelSkin.addEventListener(MouseEvent.CLICK, onHeaderClick);
  }

  private function onHeaderClick(event:MouseEvent):void {
    if (event.currentTarget is PanelSkin) {
      var ps:PanelSkin = PanelSkin(event.currentTarget);
      if (event.localY < 30) {
        dispatchEvent(new Event("headerClick"));
      }
    }
  }
```

❶

❷

❸

```
]]></fx:Script>
  <s:layout>
    <s:VerticalLayout paddingLeft="10" paddingTop="10"
      paddingBottom="10" paddingRight="10"/>
  </s:layout>
</s:Panel>
```

❶ We create metadata that declares that the HPanel class dispatches an Event named headerClick. By doing this, we can use this in MXML saying headerClick="doSomething(event)" in code which uses this component.

❷ We add an EventListener to the PanelSkin class that listens for mouse click events. Note that there's nothing magical about the name onCreationComplete—I could've called it handleCreationComplete or peterIsVerbose just as easily.

❸ When a mouse click happens, we check that the event currentTarget is a PanelSkin and that the y value of the mouse is within the header's height. (Exercise for the reader: this isn't very robust! Come up with an example of where this simple check won't work.)

❹ We add a VerticalLayout with 10-pixel padding for its border, to save ourselves effort in the Tester app.

Next, we create the Tester app that listens to the HPanel headerClick events and reacts accordingly.

session17/src/Tester.mxml

```
<?xml version="1.0" encoding="utf-8"?>
<s:Application xmlns:fx="http://ns.adobe.com/mxml/2009"
  xmlns:s="library://ns.adobe.com/flex/spark"
  xmlns:mx="library://ns.adobe.com/flex/halo"
  xmlns:comp="components.*" width="100%" height="100%">
<fx:Script><![CDATA[
  private function toggleState(newState:String):void {
    currentState = (currentState == newState) ? '' : newState;
  }
]]></fx:Script>
  <s:layout><s:BasicLayout/></s:layout>
  <s:states>
    <s:State name="default"/>
```

```
      <s:State name="stateOne"
        stateGroups="[noStateTwo, noStateThree]"/>                    ③
      <s:State name="stateTwo"
        stateGroups="[noStateOne, noStateThree]"/>
      <s:State name="stateThree"
        stateGroups="[noStateOne, noStateTwo]"/>
   </s:states>                                                         ④
   <comp:HPanel id="stateOnePanel" title="State One Panel"
     left="10" top="10" width="200" right.stateOne="10"
     height="100" bottom.stateOne="10" excludeFrom="noStateOne"
     headerClick="toggleState('stateOne')">
      <s:Label=" 松尾 芭蕉 " fontSize="20"
        fontSize.stateOne="140"/>                                     ⑤
   </comp:HPanel>
   <comp:HPanel id="stateTwoPanel" title="State Two Panel"
     left="10" bottom="10" top="115" top.stateTwo="10"               ⑥
     width="200" right.stateTwo="10" excludeFrom="noStateTwo"
     headerClick="toggleState('stateTwo')">
      <s:Label width="100%" height="100%" fontStyle="italic"
        text="(I am trusting that the following pages
http://en.wikipedia.org/wiki/Matsuo_Bash%C5%8D
and http://en.wikisource.org/wiki/Frog_Poem
have the Kanji of Matsuo Basho's name and
famous poem correct.)"/>
   </comp:HPanel>                                                     ⑦
   <comp:HPanel id="stateThreePanel" title="State Three Panel"
     excludeFrom="noStateThree" top="10"
     left="220" left.stateThree="10" right="10" bottom="10"
     headerClick="toggleState('stateThree')">                        ⑧
      <s:Label fontSize="50" fontSize.stateThree="70"
        text=" 古池や &#13; 蛙飛びこむ &#13; 水の音 "/>
      <s:Label text="--Matsuo Basho&#13;&#13;
The ancient pond&#13;A frog leaps in&#13;The sound of the water.
&#13;--Donald Keene"/>
   </comp:HPanel>
</s:Application>
```

① The `toggleState` function switches states to either the default state (which happens to be named `default`) or to the `newState` based on the value of the `currentState`. If the `currentState` is equal to the `newState`, the user has already switched to `stateOne`, `stateTwo`, or `stateThree`, so we want to switch back to the `default` state. Otherwise, we want to switch to the `newState` (which is `stateOne`, `stateTwo`, or `stateThree`).

❷ The first state is the `default` state. Naming it `default` is a convention you will sometimes encounter, but it's not a requirement.

❸ States can also belong to one or more `stateGroups`. We're using them to define `stateOne` as a state in which the `stateTwoPanel` and `stateThreePanel` aren't shown. This way, we can use `excludeFrom`. (This is a bit contrived, since I could've also just used `includeIn`, but I wanted to show both `excludeFrom` and `includeIn`, as well as `stateGroups`.)

❹ The `stateOnePanel` is at the top left, with the title "State One Panel" and the Kanji of Matsuo Basho's name (Matsuo being the family name). The `stateOne` view state is the state in which the `stateOnePanel` is expanded to take up the full app size, minus a 10-pixel border. We do this by defining the default height as 100 but the `bottom.stateOne` as 10, meaning that in `stateOne` the component is stretched so that its bottom is only 10 pixels from the bottom of the app. (I've had mixed success using `percentHeight` and `percentWidth` in conjunction with normal height and width using view states; this is a more effective way of doing this.) Finally, when learning how to use percentage sizing like `percentWidth` and `percentHeight`; constraint-based-layout like `top`, `bottom`, `left`, and `right`; and absolute positioning, there's no better way to learn than making a toy app with a few `Panels` in it and experimenting with the layouts. Please think of this app as a good basis for your own experiments.

❺ Yes, you can actually paste Kanji into Flex 4 source code!

❻ The `stateTwoPanel` is the bottom left (when in the default state) or the full app size (in the `stateTwo` state).

❼ The `stateThreePanel` is on the right (when in the default state) or the full app size (in the `stateThree` state).

❽ The  entity is used to insert newlines.

View states, which are vastly improved in Flex 4, are an easy way of making your app dynamic. They also show the importance of properly componentized design—although in this app we define the HPanel content all in one file, in real applications you want to build encapsulated components so that the application state logic and the component logic is separate. Also, note that view states aren't just limited to the application—components can have their own view states that you can switch between.

In the next workshop session we'll explore the basics of effects. Besides what we'll see in the next session, effects can be used to transition between view states in a more exciting way.

Key points

- View states are an easy way of making a Flex 4 application dynamic.
- Components can be resized, included, and excluded based on which view state they're in.
- To simplify the logic of including and excluding view states, states can be grouped into stateGroups.
- If you want to see some more examples of view states (both more basic and more advanced than this), see the view states chapter of the *Using Flex 4* PDF at http://livedocs.adobe.com/flex/gumbo/flex_4_usingsdk.pdf.

SESSION 18   Effects and animation

In this workshop session, you'll learn the basics of effects. While Flex applications already look very nice out of the box, another benefit they offer is that they can leverage the capabilities of the Flash Player. *(When writing a marketing sentence like that, I guess it's appropriate to say "leverage"—ick.)* One of these is its strong support for animation—when Macromedia coined the term rich Internet application they wanted to emphasize applications that went beyond the fairly static web apps people have grown accustomed to. Effects, when used extremely sparingly, are a good way of doing this.

This workshop session is a high-level overview whose goal is simple: I want to impress you with how easy it is to use effects, and I want to motivate you to pause at the end of this session to go read the following two excellent articles by Adobe's Chet Haase:

- Effects in Adobe Flex 4 beta—Part 1: Basic effects (www.adobe.com/devnet/flex/articles/flex4_effects_pt1_print.html)
- Effects in Adobe Flex 4 beta—Part 2: Advanced graphical effects (www.adobe.com/devnet/flex/articles/flex4_effects_pt2_print.html)

Seriously, as soon as you're done with this session, go read those articles. I'll wait.

Anyway, here's what we're going to build in this session:

Hmm, haven't we seen most of this before in the previous session?

Well, yes, we have seen the Panel contents—but we need to rotate something, after all. In this session we're including the ability to rotate and/or move this Panel together.

When you load the app and click Rotate, it looks like this:

Well, the rotation was nice, but the end location wasn't so good. You can also reload the app and click the Move button to move the poetry smoothly to the right, as shown in the following screenshot:

However, combining these effects makes the poetry get rotated around. We create a `Parallel` effect to do this for us in one smooth transition. These screenshots show the end result and also what it looks like in one of the frames of the transition:

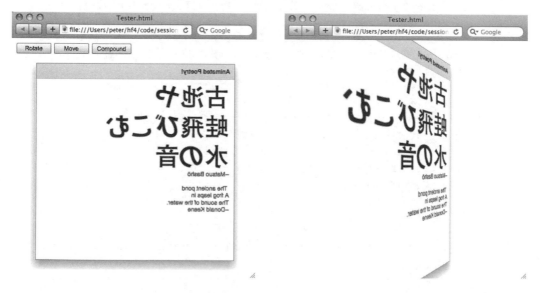

Let's look at the code. Note that we got rid of the `HPanel` and we're using just a `Panel`.

session18/src/Tester.mxml

```
<?xml version="1.0" encoding="utf-8"?>
<s:Application
  xmlns:fx="http://ns.adobe.com/mxml/2009"
  xmlns:s="library://ns.adobe.com/flex/spark"
  xmlns:mx="library://ns.adobe.com/flex/halo"
  width="100%" height="100%">                                    ❶
<fx:Declarations>                                                    ❷
  <s:Rotate3D id="rotateEffect" target="{poemPanel}"
    angleYFrom="0" angleYTo="180"/>
  <s:Move id="moveEffect" target="{poemPanel}" xBy="400"/>    ❸
  <s:Parallel id="parallelEffect" target="{poemPanel}">
    <s:Rotate3D angleYFrom="0" angleYTo="180"/>                 ❹
    <s:Move xBy="400"/>
  </s:Parallel>
</fx:Declarations>
  <s:layout>
    <s:BasicLayout/>
  </s:layout>                                                        ❺
  <s:HGroup left="10" top="10">
    <s:Button label="Rotate" click="rotateEffect.play();"/>
    <s:Button label="Move" click="moveEffect.play();"/>
    <s:Button label="Compound" click="parallelEffect.play();"/>
  </s:HGroup>
  <s:Panel id="poemPanel" title="Animated Poetry!"
    x="50" y="50" width="400" height="400">
    <s:layout>
      <s:VerticalLayout paddingTop="10" paddingLeft="10"/>
    </s:layout>
    <s:Label fontSize="50" fontSize.stateThree="70"
      text=" 古池や &#13; 蛙飛びこむ &#13; 水の音 "/>
    <s:Label text="--Matsuo Basho&#13;&#13;
The ancient pond&#13;A frog leaps in&#13;The sound of the water.
&#13;--Donald Keene"/>
  </s:Panel>
</s:Application>
```

❶ The effects are nonvisual children, so they go in an `fx:Declarations` block.

❷ The `Rotate3D` effect flips the panel on the y-axis.

❸ The `Move` effect moves the panel on the x-axis.

❹ The `Parallel` effect runs a `Rotate3D` and `Move` effect in parallel.

❺ The buttons trigger the effects.

That was easy! Note that in addition to running effects in parallel with the `Parallel` effect, you can also sequence events using a `Sequence` effect; see the API docs[2] for details.

Now, remember those articles by Chet Haase that I mentioned? Go read them. Now. No, don't check your email or Twitter—just do it.

➤ **Key points**

- Effects are nonvisual elements so they're added to an `fx:Declarations` element.

- Effects can be run in parallel using `Parallel` or sequenced using `Sequence`.

- Don't overdo it! Remember when being able to use multiple fonts in a word processor first came out, and certain people used, say, 10 of them on one page of a company newsletter? *Don't be that person.*

---

[2] http://livedocs.adobe.com/flex/gumbo/langref/mx/effects/Sequence.html#includeExamplesSummary

SESSION 19 CSS styling

In this workshop session, you'll learn how to use CSS to style a Flex 4 application. We'll see how to use CSS both inline in an MXML file and in a separate CSS file. Here's what we're going to build:

Let's see the code, starting with the Tester app.

session19/src/Tester.mxml

```
<?xml version="1.0" encoding="utf-8"?>
<s:Application
  xmlns:fx="http://ns.adobe.com/mxml/2009"
  xmlns:s="library://ns.adobe.com/flex/spark"
  xmlns:mx="library://ns.adobe.com/flex/halo"
  xmlns:comp="components.*"
  width="100%" height="100%">
<fx:Style>
  @namespace s "library://ns.adobe.com/flex/spark";
  @namespace mx "library://ns.adobe.com/flex/halo";

  s|Panel {
    color: #FF0000;
  }
```

1

2

```
    mx|Button {
      padding-left: 20;
    }
</fx:Style>
    <fx:Style source="styles.css"/>
    <s:layout>
      <s:BasicLayout/>
    </s:layout>
    <s:HGroup left="10" top="10">
      <s:Button label="A Spark Button"/>
      <mx:Button label="A Halo Button"/>
    </s:HGroup>
    <s:Panel id="poemPanel" title="Styled Poetry!"
      x="50" y="50" width="400" height="400">
      <s:layout>
        <s:VerticalLayout paddingTop="10" paddingLeft="10"/>
      </s:layout>
      <s:Label fontSize="50"
        text=" 古池や &#13; 蛙飛びこむ &#13; 水の音 "/>
      <s:Label text="--Matsuo Basho&#13;&#13;
The ancient pond&#13;A frog leaps in&#13;The sound of the water.
&#13;--Donald Keene"/>
    </s:Panel>
</s:Application>
```

❶ We need to refer to the namespaces of the Spark and Halo components when styling, so that we can style a Spark button differently than a Halo button. This makes for somewhat odd CSS, but it's much better than having Spark buttons called "FxButton."

❷ We set a Spark Panel to have a color of red.

❸ We set a Halo Button to have a paddingLeft of 20 pixels. Note that innerCap attributes have hyphenated names in CSS.

❹ We also include an external CSS file (which we'll define next).

❺ We create the two buttons that we want to style.

Next, let's look at the styles.css file.

session19/src/styles.css

```
@namespace s "library://ns.adobe.com/flex/spark";
@namespace mx "library://ns.adobe.com/flex/halo";
```

```
s|Button {
  font-weight: bold;
}

mx|Button {
  font-style: italic;
  font-size: 18;
}
```

This code listing specifies that Spark buttons have bold text and Halo buttons have 18 point italic text. Otherwise, the syntax is identical to the syntax inside an fx:Style block. This is true in general—the CSS files have the same content as Style elements.

Note that if we just had the Tester app and we commented out the reference to this external styles.css file, the app would look like this:

That's it! Besides making a subtle and calm haiku look flashy and garish, we've also used CSS—both inline in MXML files and in separate CSS files—to style Flex 4 apps!

In the last two workshop sessions, we're going to take a break from the eye candy (or, given my skills, the eye *poison*) and look at some more obscure topics: how to view the generated ActionScript 3 code, and the events dispatched during the component lifecycle.

➡ **Key points**

- Styles can be specified inline inside an fx:Style block or in external CSS files referenced by an fx:Style block. The effects of these style blocks are cumulative.
- Namespaces are used to differentiate Spark and Halo components.

SESSION 20 Peeking behind the MXML curtain

We've spent the first part of this chapter having fun and building shiny effects and styles, using the easy-to-use Spark containers. In these last two workshop sessions, the "ooh, shiny" train is going to come to a screeching halt as we take an extremely brief look at some of the internals of what's really going on in both MXML and in the component lifecycle.

These are both deep topics, which could justifiably be completely omitted from a Hello! book. Certainly, a full, gory-details explanation of them doesn't belong here. However, I don't feel comfortable just skipping them. So, I'm going to show you a preview if you will, and leave the more complete explanation to the internet.

In this workshop session, we'll take a brief peek behind the curtain of magic that is MXML. We're going to write a trivially simple app, shown here.

session20/src/Tester.mxml

```
<?xml version="1.0" encoding="utf-8"?>
<s:Application
  xmlns:fx="http://ns.adobe.com/mxml/2009"
  xmlns:s="library://ns.adobe.com/flex/spark"
  xmlns:mx="library://ns.adobe.com/flex/halo"
  width="100%" height="100%">
  <s:TextInput x="5" y="5" id="sourceTI"/>
  <s:TextInput x="5" y="30" id="destTI" text="{sourceTI.text}"/>
</s:Application>
```

All this app does is bind the text of the destTI to the text of the sourceTI, as shown in the following screenshot.

A lot of code is generated for us to make this happen. How does this all work? Well, a full explanation is beyond the scope of this book, but I want to point you in the right direction.

First, you can set a compiler flag to keep the ActionScript 3 code that's generated by the MXML compiler—recall that MXML is first converted to ActionScript 3 by the MXML compiler, and then this ActionScript 3 code is compiled into a SWF. So, let's set the flag to keep this code around and take a look at it. (Thanks to Peter DeHaan's blog[3] for this knowledge, which works the same in Flex 4 as it does in his Flex 3 example.)

Right-click on the session20 project and choose Properties. Then, choose the Flex Compiler option, and add –keep to the additonal compiler arguments, as shown in the following screenshot:

3   http://blog.flexexamples.com/2008/08/02/viewing-a-flex-applications-generated-source-code/

The next time the project is compiled, there will be a generated folder created under your src folder. Take a look at src/generated/Tester-generated.as, _Tester_FlexInit-generated.as, _Tester-binding-generated.as, and _TesterWatcherSetupUtil.as if you want to see what your Tester app turned into.

Another thing to do is to set a breakpoint (by double-clicking in the margin) on the line with the binding, and then run the app in the debugger by choosing Run > Debug > Tester (or by clicking the icon of the bug in the toolbar). You can then spelunk through all the data binding code in the Flex SDK to your heart's content. This will give you some appreciation of how much code is involved in the implementation of the Binding mechanism, and why it's worth keeping that overhead in mind for large, complicated user interfaces as a potential source of performance problems.

Finally, I'll remind you of the one-hour "Diving in the Flex Data Binding Waters"[4] presentation by Michael Labriola. Go watch it now if you haven't already done so.

➤➤ Key points

- ○ Flex, and especially data binding, isn't magic—a lot of code is involved.

- ○ One of the best ways to learn how to code Flex after you've graduated beyond the introductory books is to read the SDK source.

- ○ An easy way to read the SDK source is to debug into the files, or to just open them. You can Command-click on any of the framework classes that you're using in your source code (or right-click and choose Goto Definition, or [on Windows] type F3 when the cursor is on a class name).

---

[4] http://www.slideshare.net/michael.labriola/diving-in-the-flex-data-binding-waters-presentation?src=embed

SESSION 21 The Spark component lifecycle

Having just spent the previous session digging around in generated code, in this workshop session—the last of this chapter—we'll take a brief look at the Flex 4 component lifecycle.

First, one of the reasons that this session can be brief is that there are some really good resources online. First, there is the white-paper[5] on the new component lifecycle. Second, Brad Umbaugh and R.J. Owen of EffectiveUI posted some great slides[6] about the Flex lifecycle, which is essential reading. (I first saw a version of this talk delivered by Doug Schmidt, also of EffectiveUI, at the Vancouver Flash Platform Meetup Group.) Also, Mrinal Wadhwa posted slides from a presentation[7] about the Flex 4 component lifecycle. Both presentation references Ted Patrick's famous "Elastic Racetrack" post[8] about the workings of the Flash Player from four years ago, which is still conceptually useful today (even though the internals of the Flash Player have changed since then).

AS RJ OWEN'S PRESENTATION SAYS, COMPONENTS GO THROUGH THREE PHASES IN THE COMPONENT LIFECYCLE:
1. BIRTH
2. LIFE
3. DEATH.
EACH OF THESE HAS ITS OWN SET OF EVENTS THAT GET DISPATCHED, THAT YOU CAN HANDLE TO DO WHAT YOUR APPLICATION NEEDS TO DO.

I recommend you put this book down and go follow those links (and follow your nose from there), either right now or at the end of this session.

In this session we'll build a tiny app that shows a number of different events that happen when a component is created and destroyed. This way, you know that they're there and that you can handle them. This is a complex topic that could be the subject of several book chapters if covered thoroughly; we'll stick with the basics here. (This isn't "Rome in a Day," it's "Rome in an Hour, on a Vespa.")

---

[5] http://opensource.adobe.com/wiki/display/flexsdk/Gumbo+Component+Architecture#GumboComponentArchitecture-NewComponentLifecycle

[6] www.slideshare.net/rjowen/adobe-flex-component-lifecycle-presentation

[7] http://weblog.mrinalwadhwa.com/2009/06/21/flex-4-component-lifecycle

[8] www.onflex.org/ted/2005/07/flash-player-mental-model-elastic.php

In this session we're going to build the following application:

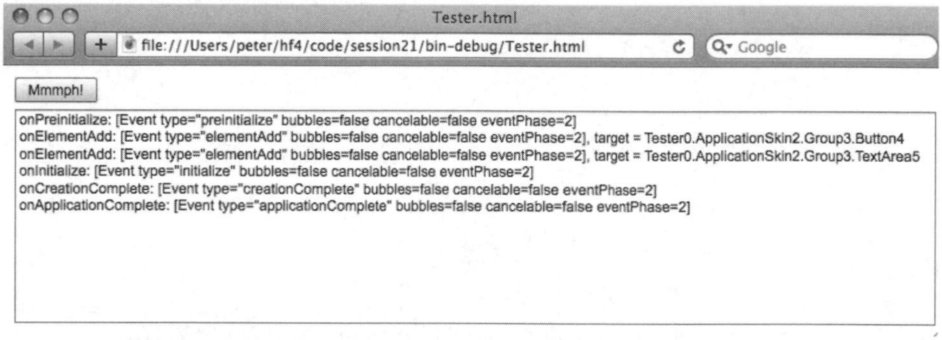

Clicking the button removes it and triggers the `elementRemove` event, as shown in the following screenshot (note the last line in the `TextArea`).

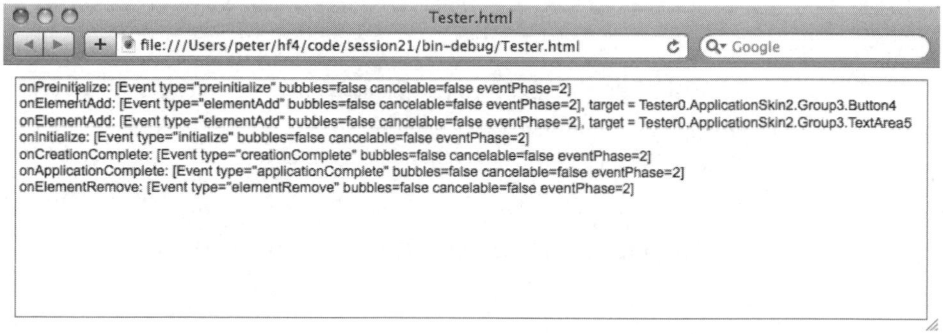

So, let's see the code.

session21/src/Tester.mxml

```
<?xml version="1.0" encoding="utf-8"?>
<s:Application
  xmlns:fx="http://ns.adobe.com/mxml/2009"
  xmlns:s="library://ns.adobe.com/flex/spark"
  xmlns:mx="library://ns.adobe.com/flex/halo"
  preinitialize="onPreinitialize(event)"
  initialize="onInitialize(event)"
  creationComplete="onCreationComplete(event)"
  elementAdd="onElementAdd(event)"
  elementRemove="onElementRemove(event)"
  applicationComplete="onApplicationComplete(event)"
```

❶

```
    width="100%" height="100%">
<fx:Script><![CDATA[
  import spark.events.ElementExistenceEvent;
  import mx.events.FlexEvent;

  [Bindable]                                                          2
  private var _text:String = "";

  protected function onPreinitialize(event:FlexEvent):void {
    _text += "onPreinitialize: " + event + "\n";
  }

  protected function onInitialize(event:FlexEvent):void {
    _text += "onInitialize: " + event + "\n";
  }

  protected function onCreationComplete(event:FlexEvent):void {
    _text += "onCreationComplete: " + event + "\n";
  }

  protected function onApplicationComplete(
  event:FlexEvent):void {
    _text += "onApplicationComplete: " + event + "\n";
  }

  protected function onElementAdd(event:ElementExistenceEvent):
  void {
    _text += "onElementAdd: " + event + ", target = " +
      event.element + "\n";
  }
  protected function onElementRemove(
  event:ElementExistenceEvent):void {
    _text += "onElementRemove: " + event + "\n";
  }
]]></fx:Script>
  <s:layout>
    <s:VerticalLayout paddingLeft="10" paddingTop="10"
      paddingRight="10" paddingBottom="10"/>
  </s:layout>
  <s:Button id="kenny" label="Mmmph!"                        3
    click="removeElement(kenny)"/>
  <s:TextArea id="debugTA" text="{_text}" width="100%"
    height="100%"/>                                               4
</s:Application>
```

❶ We add handlers for the different events dispatched by the application. The applicationComplete event is defined by the Application class; the rest are inherited from the UIComponent class. Again, there's nothing special about the onPreinitialize function name; onFooBar is just a naming convention for functions that handle foo-Bar events.

❷ We create a bindable _text variable to store debugging information in. We don't just set the debugTA text directly, since the preinitialize Event happens before the debugTA even exists! (Try it and see your app explode. I'm serious: do this. You can learn a lot about Flex by trying to deliberately break your applications and see what happens in the traces when you succeed—and in learning what happens when something you think will break a Flex app doesn't.)

❸ Clicking the kenny button calls the removeElement method of the application (inherited from SkinnableContainer) to remove the kenny button.

❹ The debugTA TextArea has its text property bound to the _text variable.

That's it!

Running the app, we see the events printed in the order in which they occur. We see that preinitialize happens before the Button and the TextArea are added to the app, and that the initialize, creationComplete, and applicationComplete events then take place.

➤ Key points

- A number of events are broadcast when Flex components are created and removed. These events can bubble up the component containment hierarchy when their bubbles property is set to true. Events can also contain custom data, as you'll see in chapter 7 when we build a full Flex application using the Cairngorm application framework for Flex.

- To understand the component lifecycle in depth, go to www.slideshare.net/rjowen/adobe-flex-component-lifecycle-presentation.

What's next?

This chapter has been a whirlwind tour of Spark containers, layouts, view states, and CSS styling, as well as a brief glance at some complex topics that need chapters longer than this one all to themselves to be fully understood.

In the next chapter we're going to switch gears from Spark and look at Halo. Recall that in Session 5 we looked briefly at Halo? You probably got the sense that there was this whole other way of writing Flex 4 apps, but that it was somewhat quaint and that we didn't want to talk about it. Well, in Flex 4 it turns out that Halo is still relevant after all. In the next chapter we'll take a tour of some of the Halo components that are still relevant to you as a Flex 4 developer—either they don't have Spark equivalents or they're more functional in some important way than their current Spark equivalents.

Chances are you'll be using this subset of Halo components every day—*OK, well, maybe every other day*—as a Flex 4 developer, so the next chapter is essential information.

5

Halo Flex 4: Using DataGrid, Navigator Containers, and Popups

W ay back in Session 5 we discussed that there was a namepsace (`library://ns.adobe.com/flex/halo`) full of the old Halo components that were used in Flex 1 through Flex 3. I showed an example of an app built using only Halo components. It was simple, featuring containers like `HBox` and `Panel` and controls like `List` and `Button`. Since they're in a different namespace, these `Panel`, `List`, and `Button` classes are different from the Spark ones. This separate namespace is a bit awkward at first but is far preferable to the original idea, which was to use a horrible `Fx` prefix on the new Spark components.

AH, HALO. THIS IS A SENTIMENTAL SET OF WORKSHOP SESSIONS FOR ME, SINCE WHEN I WAS LEARNING THE HALO COMPONENTS IT WAS 2004, I HAD JUST STARTED A NEW JOB AND MY SON WAS TWO MONTHS OLD...

WOW, WHAT A LOT OF NOSTALGIC NONSENSE. YOU SOUND LIKE AN OLD MAN. I'M THE OLD MAN HERE SONNY, GET OFF MY LAWN!

We left Halo at that point and we haven't revisited it—until now. In this chapter we'll take a tour of some of the Halo components that are still relevant to you as a Flex 4 developer. By *still relevant*, I mean that they either don't have Spark equivalents or that they're more functional in some important way than their current Spark equivalents. Although you can read a lot of articles about this topic, one masterful article stands out as far superior to the others: Joan Lafferty's "Differences between Flex 3 and Flex 4 beta."[1] Joan is the Flex SDK Quality Lead, and that article is not only authoritative but also extremely readable.

Anyway, regarding the tour of Halo components we're taking in this chapter: we'll be hitting the highlights only. So it isn't an exhaustive tour; it's more like a "Halo in a Day" kind of tour. We'll be skipping Halo components like the AdvancedDataGrid, which are too, ahem, advanced for a "Hello" book. We'll also be skipping components like Tree, Menu, and MenuBar, which are used less often and also are well documented in the online API docs.[2]

So, what *are* we going to cover? First, we'll explore classes such as DataGrid that have no Spark equivalents and that are still essential tools in the Flex 4 developer's tool belt. Next, we'll cover the Halo navigator containers, since they're still very handy and simple to use in cases where you don't mind your Flex app looking like a Flex app. (Also, there's a lot of Flex 2 and Flex 3 code in existence, so even if you're not going to use these navigator containers in new code you should understand how they work.) Finally, we'll describe how to create pop-up windows using the PopUpManager, and we'll see how to use the Alert class.

By the end of this chapter, you should know what Halo options are available to you if the Spark solution isn't working out the way you want it to. Also, you'll understand how to use the Halo navigator containers. This is a short chapter, since I'm not trying to reproduce the API docs in this book and since the new Spark components are the preferred way of building most new components. However, at least until Flex 5, Halo should remain an important tool in your proverbial tool belt, so it's worth knowing.

FLEX 4 IS EVOLVING

This book was written using the Beta 1 version of Flex 4. However, we delayed going to press until the Beta 2 version was released in

---

[1] www.adobe.com/devnet/flex/articles/flex3and4_differences_print.html

[2] See http://livedocs.adobe.com/flex/gumbo/langref/mx/controls/Tree.html, http://livedocs.adobe.com/flex/gumbo/langref/mx/controls/Menu.html, and http://livedocs.adobe.com/flex/gumbo/langref/mx/controls/MenuBar.html for the LiveDocs for these classes.

October 2009, so that we could update any code that changed. (It's a good thing too, or there would have been s:SimpleText everywhere instead of s:Label, and the code would not have compiled!) Adobe has improved Spark for Beta 2, and presumably will continue to improve Spark before the final release of Flex 4. However, this chapter is still essential reading: most Flex developers will encounter Flex 3 (and earlier) code in their career, so understanding Halo is essential to being a skilled Flex developer. You can check manning.com/armstrong3 and helloflex4.com for updates to the book code once the final version of Flex 4 is released (estimated Q1 2010).

SESSION 22 List and DataGrid

THE HALO LIST IS STILL USEFUL, BUT THIS BOOK IS BEING WRITTEN WHILE FLEX 4 IS IN BETA. I'M NOT SURE IF THE SPARK LIST WILL HAVE WORD WRAPPING MADE EASIER BY LAUNCH...

In this workshop session, you'll learn how to use the Halo List and DataGrid classes. The Halo DataGrid class is an extremely useful way of displaying multiple-column data, as shown in the accompanying figure. Furthermore, the Halo DataGrid is without a Spark equivalent—so if you have any tabular data in your application, you need to know how to use it.

But why are we looking at the Halo List? Yes, there's a Spark List, but the Halo List is still useful since (in this Flex 4 beta version, anyway) the Spark List doesn't do word wrapping automatically, so there are cases where it's a lot easier to just use a Halo List.

First, we're going to create a Task model object to display in our Halo List and DataGrid classes.

sessionX/src/model/Task.as

```
package model {
  [Bindable]
  public class Task {
    public var name:String;
    public var notes:String;
```

```
    public var due:Date;

    public function Task(
      name:String = "", notes:String = "", due:Date = null) {      ◀─┐
      this.name = name;                                              ➋
      this.notes = notes;
      this.due = due == null ? new Date() : due;
    }
  }
}
```

I'm introducing something new here, and marking the `Task` class itself as `Bindable` ➊, instead of the individual properties. Using this annotation on the class makes all of the properties in the class `Bindable`. Why didn't I show you this before? Simple: it's too tempting to abuse, since it saves typing. Since `Bindable` properties have considerable runtime overhead, you need to really use this annotation sparingly. Furthermore, even if it makes sense for the properties you have on a class, the maintenance programmer who inherits your class may very well add properties that should not be `Bindable`. If this happens, will he or she really remove the annotation and add it to all the individual properties?

So: don't use [Bindable] on a class as a lazy shortcut in anything but the smallest of apps!

The `Task` class has a constructor that sets all the properties with any of the optional parameters ➋ passed in. By now, this code should be straightforward.

Next, we create a Tester app that illustrates the use of the Halo `List` and `DataGrid`, as promised. Our app looks like this:

Note that the List on the left has nice alternating row colors, rows that have variable height and word wrapping. The DataGrid on the right has nicely formatted dates and sortable columns (just click on their headers). Be advised that sorting the DataGrid sorts the underlying ArrayCollection, which affects the List as well. If you want sortability without affecting the ArrayCollection, you can wrap its source Array in a ListCollectionView object (or in another ArrayCollection), so sorting will apply to that new ArrayCollection and not to this ArrayCollection.

Anyway, let's look at the code.

sessionX/src/Tester.mxml

```xml
<?xml version="1.0" encoding="utf-8"?>
<s:Application
  xmlns:fx="http://ns.adobe.com/mxml/2009"
  xmlns:s="library://ns.adobe.com/flex/spark"
  xmlns:mx="library://ns.adobe.com/flex/halo"
  width="100%" height="100%">
<fx:Script>
<![CDATA[
  import mx.collections.ArrayCollection;
  import model.Task;

  [Bindable]
  private var _tasks:ArrayCollection = new ArrayCollection([      ❶
    new Task("Learn Flex 4", "This book is helping!"),
    new Task("Lose weight", "Exercise? Fad diet? Both?"),
    new Task("Buy groceries", "Including vegetables this time!"),
    new Task("Eat"), new Task("Drink"), new Task("Be Merry")]);

  private function formatTask(task:Task):String {            ❷
    return task.name +
    (task.notes == "" ? "" : (" (" + task.notes + ")")) +
    ", due on " + dateFormatter.format(task.due) + ".";
  }

  private function formatDate(item:Object,               ❸
    column:DataGridColumn):String
  {
    var task:Task = item as Task;
    return task == null ? "" : dateFormatter.format(task.due);
```

```
    }
]]></fx:Script>
<fx:Declarations>                                                          ④
    <mx:DateFormatter id="dateFormatter" formatString="YYYY-MM-DD"/>   ←┘
</fx:Declarations>
    <s:layout>
        <s:HorizontalLayout paddingLeft="10" paddingTop="10"
            paddingBottom="10" paddingRight="10"/>
    </s:layout>                                                            ⑤
    <mx:List dataProvider="{_tasks}" labelFunction="formatTask"        ←┘
        alternatingItemColors="[#EEEEEE, #FFFFFF]"
        variableRowHeight="true" wordWrap="true"
        width="250" height="150"/>                                         ⑥
    <mx:DataGrid width="100%" height="150" dataProvider="{_tasks}">    ←┘
        <mx:columns>
            <mx:DataGridColumn headerText="Name" dataField="name"
                width="150"/>
            <mx:DataGridColumn headerText="Due" dataField="due"            ⑦
                width="100" labelFunction="formatDate"/>               ←┘
            <mx:DataGridColumn headerText="Notes" dataField="notes"/>
        </mx:columns>
    </mx:DataGrid>
</s:Application>
```

This code creates an ArrayCollection of Tasks ❶ and assigns it to _tasks. This ArrayCollection is used by both the Halo List ❺ and DataGrid ❻ classes, so changes to its sort (made when clicking on the DataGrid header) affect both views. Next, we create formatTask ❷ and formatDate ❸ functions, which are the labelFunctions of the List ❺, and the Due column ❼ of the DataGrid respectively. These functions are responsible for formatting whatever data from the individual row in the data provider is desired into a string that will be presented in the DataGrid column or List. Finally, note the use of a DateFormatter ❹ to format dates—and that it uses the unambiguous YYYY-MM-DD format, not the MM/DD/YYYY format, which is mistakable for DD/MM/YYYY. The next chapter covers formatters at great length, so for now just know that formatters are useful components that simplify the task of formatting data.

That's it! We've seen how to use the Halo List and DataGrid. Given what the DataGrid class in particular accomplishes, there's remarkably little code to write.

➤ Key points

- ○ The Halo `List` is still useful, since out of the box it's nicer than the Spark `List` for common cases where you just want to display text nicely. (It's less customizable, however, and will probably eventually be obsolete.)

- ○ The Halo `DataGrid` is an extremely useful way of showing multicolumn data. Actually, since there's no Spark equivalent, it's the only way.

- ○ Both the `List` and `DataGridColumns` can have `labelFunctions` that can format their data nicely. Note the different method signatures required, however.

SESSION 23 TabNavigator, ViewStack, and Accordion

In this workshop session, we'll continue our tour of Halo. Having discussed some of the most useful Halo controls, let's now switch gears and take a tour of the Halo navigator containers. As of Flex 4 Beta 1, there are no direct Spark equivalents for these either, and frankly, I miss them. Presumably this is because the new improved view state syntax means that view states are a lot more usable now than they were, so you can just roll your own. In many ways, it's a shame there's no Spark equivalent for these containers (even one implemented using view states), since many times you don't care about being funky and custom and you just want some tabs.

YES, IT'S TRUE THAT THE NEW SPARK COMPONENTS ARE MORE FLEXIBLE THAN THE HALO ONES, AND THAT YOU CAN MAKE YOUR UI LOOK HOW YOU WANT TO EASIER, BUT SOMETIMES YOU JUST WANT A TAB NAVIGATOR... *SNIFF*

So, in this section you'll learn what's arguably the most straightforward way to rapidly create the layout and navigational flow of a Flex 4 application: using Halo navigator containers. As you read the code, you'll probably be struck by how simple and elegant it is. If only tabs were allowed to always look like tabs…

Keep in mind that using these Halo containers is less customizable by your designer than just using Spark throughout, so using these Halo containers may not always be appropriate. Furthermore, they'll presumably be deprecated in some future version of Flex, so choose wisely.

Anyway, what we're building looks like the following screen:

Clicking the `Accordion` button in the `LinkBar` selects the `Accordion` child of the `ViewStack`, shown here. An `Accordion` is like the Microsoft Outlook bar, which shows one child at a time, has a vertical orientation, and shows a nice smooth animated transition when switching between children. The cool factor makes up for the slight waste of space, but the `Accordion` shouldn't have too many children or there's no space for the actual content of each.

NO WAY, I WANT TO MAKE BUTTONS IN PHOTOSHOP, DROP THEM INTO FLASH CATALYST, AND HAVE THE FLEX DEVELOPERS USE THEM. I NEVER WANT THE STANDARD TABS. EVER.

And without further ado, let's see the code.

session23/src/Tester.mxml

```
<?xml version="1.0" encoding="utf-8"?>
<s:Application
  xmlns:fx="http://ns.adobe.com/mxml/2009"
```

```
  xmlns:s="library://ns.adobe.com/flex/spark"
  xmlns:mx="library://ns.adobe.com/flex/halo"
  width="100%" height="100%"
  initialize="init()">
  <s:layout>
    <s:VerticalLayout paddingLeft="10" paddingTop="10"
      paddingRight="10" paddingBottom="10"/>
  </s:layout>
  <mx:Panel width="100%" height="100%" title="I See Your Halo...">
    <mx:LinkBar dataProvider="{vs}" width="100%"/>              <-- ❶
    <mx:ViewStack id="vs" width="100%" height="100%">           <-- ❷
      <mx:TabNavigator width="100%" height="100%" paddingLeft="5"  <--
        label="Tab Navigator">                                         ❸
        <mx:VBox label="One" width="100%" height="100%">
          <mx:Label text="Here's a button:"/>
          <mx:Button label="A Halo Button"/>
        </mx:VBox>
        <mx:VBox label="Two" width="100%" height="100%">
          <mx:Label text="Shameless self-promotion:"/>
          <mx:Image
source="http://www.manning.com/armstrong/armstrong_cover150.jpg"/> <--
        </mx:VBox>                                                       ❹
        <mx:VBox label="Three" width="100%" height="100%">
          <mx:Label text="Stuff inside Three"/>
        </mx:VBox>
      </mx:TabNavigator>
      <mx:Accordion width="100%" height="100%" label="Accordion">  <--
        <mx:VBox label="Four" width="100%" height="100%">               ❺
          <mx:Label text="Stuff inside Four"/>
        </mx:VBox>
        <mx:VBox label="Five" width="100%" height="100%">
          <mx:Label text="Stuff inside Five"/>
        </mx:VBox>
        <mx:VBox label="Six" width="100%" height="100%">
          <mx:Label text="Stuff inside Six"/>
        </mx:VBox>
      </mx:Accordion>
    </mx:ViewStack>
  </mx:Panel>
</s:Application>
```

The LinkBar ❶ has its dataProvider set to the ViewStack ❷, meaning
that the LinkButtons are created based on the label attributes of the

TabNavigator ❸ and Accordion ❺ children of the ViewStack ❷. Finally, note that the mx:Image ❹ can have its source be a URL, even an external site on the internet.

WARNING   The Halo TabNavigator and Accordion contained VBox children. There's actually an underlying requirement here: Halo navigator containers (like ViewStack, TabNavigator, and Accordion) *can only contain Halo container children* (like VBox, HBox, Box, or Canvas). You can't stick a Spark Group directly inside one of them, just like you can't stick a Spark or Halo TextInput directly inside one of them.

We've seen how the Halo navigator containers are useful and simple to use. However, they require Halo container children, which is worth keeping in mind. That, along with the fact that they're harder to skin, means that for applications where visual design is important and where "looks like a Flex app" is a bug instead of a feature, the Spark view states and Groups are probably a safer bet in the long run despite the added effort. Still, it's good to know how to use the Halo navigator components: sometimes a tab is just a tab.

➡ Key points

- The ViewStack, TabNavigator, and Accordion containers each show only one of their children at a time. The difference is the way you navigate between them, hence "navigator" containers.

- The labels shown in the ViewStack, TabNavigator, and Accordion containers are derived from the label property of the Halo containers they contain.

- Using a LinkBar in conjunction with a ViewStack is typical. A LinkBar can have a direction of either horizontal (the default) or vertical.

SESSION 24 Alert.show and the PopupManager

WELL, WHAT ABOUT TITLE WINDOWS? DO YOU MIND THOSE LOOKING LIKE EVERYBODY ELSE'S TITLE WINDOWS?

In this workshop session, you'll learn how to use the PopUpManager to show TitleWindows. When a TitleWindow is used with its modal property set to true, the combination gives your application the equivalent of the "lightbox" effect you see Web 2.0 applications using in JavaScript, in which the underlying UI is dimmed and disabled. (Of course, the ironic thing is that those applications are imitating a desktop UI paradigm.)

Continuing the modal goodness, we'll see how to use Alert.show to display short modal messages to the user. Alert.show is the refuge of both UI scoundrels and developers who can't be bothered to learn how to use either the debugger or trace statements.

As an added bonus, I'll show you the Halo RichTextEditor, since it's an efficient way of editing rich text and since there's no Spark equivalent. (Of course, the HTML code that it outputs leaves a lot to be desired; to fix this, you can subclass it and override this behavior using an approach found at http://code.google.com/p/flex-richtexteditor-html-utils/.)

In this workshop session, we're going to build an Application that has two Buttons. The first one shows an Alert box; the second one shows a TitleWindow, as you can see here:

Closing the `TitleWindow` by clicking on the X will set the text of a `RichEd-itableText` Spark control (I chose it for variety; we could've used a `Label`) to the HTML produced by the `RichTextEditor`. You can see this in the following screenshot:

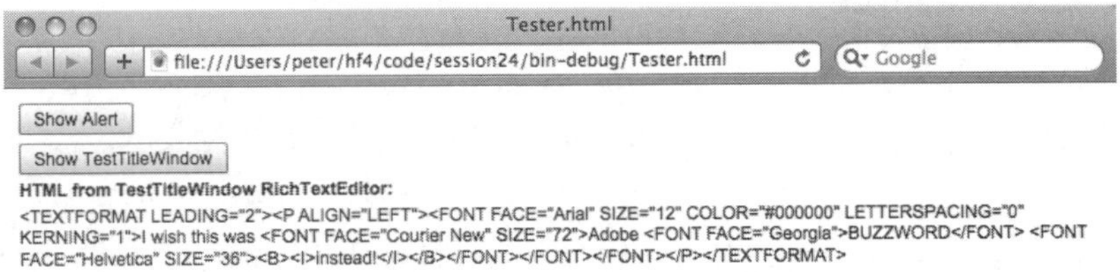

Finally, when clicked the Show Alert button shows an `Alert` dialog:

Enough talking! Let's see the code.

session24/src/Tester.mxml

```
<?xml version="1.0" encoding="utf-8"?>
<s:Application
  xmlns:fx="http://ns.adobe.com/mxml/2009"
  xmlns:s="library://ns.adobe.com/flex/spark"
  xmlns:mx="library://ns.adobe.com/flex/halo"
  width="100%" height="100%"
  initialize="init()">
<fx:Script><![CDATA[
  import mx.events.CloseEvent;
  import mx.controls.Alert;
  import mx.managers.PopUpManager;

  private function showAlert(event:MouseEvent):void {          ❶
    Alert.show('That was easy!', 'Alert!');
  }
```

```
private function showPopUp(event:MouseEvent):void {
  var titleWindow:TestTitleWindow = TestTitleWindow(
    PopUpManager.createPopUp(this, TestTitleWindow, true));     ←──┐
  titleWindow.x = 50;                                             ❷
  titleWindow.y = 50;
  titleWindow.addEventListener(CloseEvent.CLOSE, onCloseTTW);  ←──┐

}                                                                 ❸


private function onCloseTTW(event:CloseEvent):void {
  var ttw:TestTitleWindow = TestTitleWindow(event.target);
  richEditableText.text = ttw.richTextEditor.htmlText;       ←──┐
}                                                             ❹
]]></fx:Script>
  <s:layout>
    <s:VerticalLayout paddingLeft="10" paddingTop="10"
      paddingRight="10" paddingBottom="10"/>
  </s:layout>
  <s:Button label="Show Alert" click="showAlert(event)"/>
  <s:Button label="Show TestTitleWindow" click="showPopUp(event)"/>
  <s:Label text="HTML from TestTitleWindow RichTextEditor:"
    fontWeight="bold"/>
  <s:RichEditableText id="richEditableText" width="100%"
    height="100%"/>
</s:Application>
```

❶ Alert.show takes parameters for the text, title, and other values.

❷ PopUpManager.createPopUp shows a TitleWindow and returns a refer-ence to the new instance. The third constructor parameter specifies whether it's modal. Note that the popup doesn't get displayed right away—you can add the event listeners and position things, all without worrying that there will be display artifacts. This is unique to the Flex/Flash architecture and may surprise you if you have a background in other UI frameworks.

❸ We add the onCloseTTW function as an EventListener for the CloseEvent, which is triggered when the user clicks the close box on the window frame.

❹ We set the text property of the richEditableText to the htmlText property of the RichTextEditor.

NO. BUT, OF COURSE
I'D NEVER USE THEM.
DUDE, THE 80S CALLED,
IT WANTS ITS UI
METAPHORS BACK.
JUST SAYIN'...

Note that while `Alert.show` ❶ is quick and easy, using `PopUpManager.createPopUp` ❷ requires having a subclass of `TitleWindow` to show. Also, note that as a habit we cast the instance that's returned by `createPopUp` to the specific class—in our case `TestTitleWindow`—because then we can set its properties easier. (The `createPopUp` method returns an `IFlexDisplayObject`, which may not have the properties you need to set.) The `onClos-eTTW` ❹ function is added as an `EventListener` ❸ for the `CloseEvent` that's triggered when the window frame close button (the little X in the top-right corner) is clicked.

Finally, we create the `TestTitleWindow` subclass of `TitleWindow`.

sessionX/src/TestTitleWindow.mxml

```
<?xml version="1.0" encoding="utf-8"?>
<mx:TitleWindow xmlns:fx="http://ns.adobe.com/mxml/2009"
  xmlns:s="library://ns.adobe.com/flex/spark"
  xmlns:mx="library://ns.adobe.com/flex/halo"
  layout="vertical" title="TestTitleWindow"
  width="600" height="400" showCloseButton="true"
  close="PopUpManager.removePopUp(this);">            ⟵——┐
  <fx:Script>                                              ❶
    <![CDATA[
      import mx.managers.PopUpManager;
    ]]>
  </fx:Script>
  <s:Group width="100%">
    <s:Label text="You can put a lot in a TitleWindow!"/>
  </s:Group>
  <mx:RichTextEditor id="richTextEditor" width="100%" height="100%"/> ❷
</mx:TitleWindow>
```

❶ Set showCloseButton to get the window frame close button, and handle the close Event to close the TitleWindow. Since all I want to do is call the PopUpManager.removePopUp method, I just put the method call as the value of the close attribute, and the appropriate handler is created. *(Yes, that's cool. My copy editor couldn't believe I was handling the event either.)*

❷ The `RichTextEditor` is nice, but if you work with it for a while you'll wish it was nicer (like, say, Buzzword).

The `TestTitleWindow` uses the `PopUpManager.removePopUp` method **❶** to close itself when the window frame close button is clicked. The `RichTextEditor` instance sticks around when closed, so we can get its `htmlText` **❷**.

As you've seen, dropping in a `RichTextEditor` requires very little code. Also, note that we can use Spark `Group`s as well as Halo components inside the `TitleWindow` container.

➤ Key points

- The `PopUpManager` can show `TitleWindow` subclasses, which you typically define in MXML.
- `Alert.show` is a quick and easy way to show modal dialog messages.

What's next?

This was a quick tour through the most important Halo components that have no Spark equivalents. If you work in a company that employs a lot of designers, it could very well be that the only Halo component you use regularly is the `DataGrid`. Most of the other Halo components we've seen in this chapter have Spark alternatives, but for displaying tabular data in Flex the `DataGrid` is the only viable option. However, if you're building apps that are allowed to look like Flex apps (especially internal apps for, say, company intranets), you'll find that the Halo navigator containers are a good choice for the navigation within your Flex 4 apps.

In the next chapter, we'll switch gears a bit and cover Flex forms, including how to use formatters and validators. Like it or not, almost everyone building Flex applications ends up building a lot of forms, so understanding how formatters and validators work is essential. Furthermore, the way that Flex forms are laid out is still done using two specialized Halo layout containers that we didn't discuss in this chapter: `Form` and `FormItem`. So, in chapter 6 we'll describe how to use those as well, and Halo's relevance lives on…

6

Building user-friendly forms using Flex formatters and validators

In this chapter, you'll learn how to use the formatters and validators that make building data entry forms in Flex such a pleasure—well, at least compared to everywhere else. Flex formatters are used primarily to format data that's being displayed to the user in controls like the `DataGrid` you saw in chapter 5. Flex formatters can also be used to take user input and turn it into correctly formatted input. Flex validators are used to validate user input and display validation messages when the user input isn't correct.

The API documentation for formatters and validators is excellent in many regards; however, one area it has always been lousy at is showing how to use formatters and validators together on the same input controls that the user is using. There's a good reason for this: it's a bit tricky to do well! However, if you care about making your forms as usable as possible, this is the road you'll inevitably end up going down. So, if you do, the time this chapter could save you should alone be worth the book price.

Ever since Flex 1.0, the support for formatting has been good, and the support for validation has been better. The biggest improvement since the

early days of Flex is that validator classes can now have id properties and that you can bind to their properties. So, building apps that integrate formatting and validation on the same components is easier now than it once was.

We'll start by building a small toy example that uses the built-in Flex formatters and validators in a straightforward way. Our goal is to see how formatters and validators work without extra work on our part. Then, we'll dive in and build a full-fledged AddressForm that will show how formatters and validators can be used together in real-world situations. This task will require some effort on our part: the AddressForm is about 180 lines of code, so it's a bit more complex than the examples we've seen so far. This is fine, however: as we're concluding the stand-alone workshop sessions in this chapter, it's good to end with a bang, not a whimper. Furthermore, form code may seem boring, but it's a meal ticket for many Flex programmers. Also, there are lots of ways to shoot yourself in the foot with data binding when integrating formatting and validation, so this is a very relevant chapter.

Besides, in the next chapter we take the sustained example approach even further, spending some 40 pages building a Twitter + Yahoo! Maps mashup. So, wading through a few pages of form code will serve as an appetizer for the code feast ahead, if you wish. Finally, we'll be using the Form and FormItem Halo layout components in the AddressForm. So, we haven't seen the last of Halo.

First, however, let's build the small toy example that uses the built-in Flex formatters and validators that I promised.

SESSION 25 Formatters and validators

ACTUALLY, SID, THE WHOLE "IN THIS ECONOMY" THING IS JUST A RUNNING JOKE FOR ME. IT'S THE PERFECT ANSWER FOR ANY QUESTION. IF I'M IN THE DRIVE THROUGH AND THEY ASK "DO YOU WANT FRIES WITH THAT?", MY ANSWER IS ALWAYS "FRIES? IN *THIS* ECONOMY?"

In this workshop session, we'll start by seeing what the built-in formatters and validators in Flex can do. At this point I could launch into a huge example featuring all the standard Flex formatters and validators at once, but they essentially all function the same way (except for `CreditCardValidator`; see the API documentation for details).

All formatters are subclasses of `mx.formatters.Formatter`. The subclasses of `Formatter` that come with Flex 4 are `CurrencyFormatter`, `DateFormatter`, `NumberFormatter`, `PhoneFormatter`, and `ZipCodeFormatter`. The `Formatter` class defines a `format()` method, which must be overridden by its subclasses.

Similarly, all validators are subclasses of `mx.validators.Validator`, which implements the ability to make required the field it's validating by setting the `required` property of the `Validator` to true. The following are the different `Validator` subclasses included in Flex 4: `CreditCardValidator`, `CurrencyValidator`, `DateValidator`, `EmailValidator`, `NumberValidator`, `PhoneNumberValidator`, `RegExpValidator`, `SocialSecurityValidator`, `StringValidator`, `StyleValidator`, and `ZipCodeValidator`.

So, since they're essentially all the same, in this workshop session we'll pick one formatter and one validator to look at: `CurrencyFormatter` and `CurrrencyValidator`. I selected these since showing how they interact is straightforward, and since formatting money is something you may very well want to do. We'll build a small app that uses both on the same Spark `TextInput` class. We'll see many more formatters and validators in the next session when we build an address form.

The app we're going to build in this session looks like this when we're typing text into the `TextInput`:

Once we focus out (by pressing the Tab key), the CurrencyFormatter formats the text, resulting in the following screen:

If we type garbage into the field and focus out, we preserve the garbage in question so that our validator shows the correct message:

This is a lot of functionality, and it would take a lot of code to accomplish this in some frameworks. Let's see the Flex code for this.

session25/src/Tester.mxml

```
<?xml version="1.0" encoding="utf-8"?>
<s:Application
  xmlns:fx="http://ns.adobe.com/mxml/2009"
  xmlns:s="library://ns.adobe.com/flex/spark"
  xmlns:mx="library://ns.adobe.com/flex/halo"
  width="100%" height="100%">
<fx:Script><![CDATA[
  protected function moneyTIFocusOutHandler(event:FocusEvent):void {  ❶
    var formattedText:String =
      currencyFormatter.format(moneyTI.text);
    if (formattedText != "") {
      moneyTI.text = formattedText;                            ←  ❷
    }
  }
]]></fx:Script>
<fx:Declarations>                                             ❸
  <mx:CurrencyFormatter id="currencyFormatter"           ←
    precision="2" rounding="nearest"/>
  <mx:CurrencyValidator id="currencyValidator" precision="2"     ←
    source="{moneyTI}" property="text" triggerEvent="focusOut"/>  ❹
</fx:Declarations>
  <s:layout>
    <s:VerticalLayout paddingTop="10" paddingLeft="10"/>
  </s:layout>                                                 ❺
  <s:TextInput id="moneyTI"                              ←
    focusOut="moneyTIFocusOutHandler(event)"/>
```

```
    <s:Button label="Really, I'm just here for the focus..."/>
</s:Application>
```

1 This function formats the text on focusOut.

2 We only assign the text to the moneyTI.text if formatting succeeded.

3 The CurrencyFormatter is set to round to the nearest penny.

4 The CurrencyValidator is set to validate the text property of the moneyTI.

5 Here we handle the focusOut Event of the moneyTI TextInput.

Note that if we didn't use the guard statement **2** inside the moneyTIFo-cusOutHandler **1**, the currencyFormatter **3** would assign the text of the moneyTI **5** in all cases. This result would be less than satisfactory, since even though the CurrencyValidator **4** would show an error message, it would be the error for having typed nothing (because the CurrencyFor-matter would be triggered before the CurrencyValidator). The following screenshot shows this:

That's it! We've seen how to use formatters and validators together, and you now know that with a bit of care in checking the formatter output you can produce a very usable UI.

➤ Key points

I LIKE TO USE "THAT'S WHAT SHE SAID" AS MY RUNNING JOKE. IT'S MORE EDGY.

YOU ACTUALLY USE A SEXIST RUNNING JOKE IN THIS ECONOMY?

TOUCHÉ

THAT'S WHAT... NEVER MIND.

- Formatters are used to format text nicely.
- Validators are used to validate whether a value matches the criteria defined by the validator. Typically, they're used with TextInputs, but (as we'll see in the next session) they can also be used with things like DropDownLists.
- Formatters return the empty string when they fail, so be sure to check for that before using their value somewhere. Otherwise, you'll be validating the wrong thing.
- You can write your own custom formatters and validators, as we'll see in the next section.

SESSION 26 Real-world forms, formatters, and validators

In this workshop session, we'll dive deeper into formatters and validators, building an AddressForm that's as close to production code as you'll get in a book. Of course, in the real world things aren't as easy as in toy examples, so this workshop session won't be a toy either. We'll use a number of validators in this example, specifically a NumberValidator, RegExpValidator, StringValidator, and ZipCodeValidator. We'll also use the ZipCodeFormatter class. This table shows how we'll use these classes in this session:

Class	Purpose in this session
NumberValidator	Validating that DropDownLists have selected values
RegExpValidator	Performing customized validation of Canadian postal codes
StringValidator	Validating that the Street Address and City fields have the minimum amount of text in them
ZipCodeValidator	Validating US zip codes
ZipCodeFormatter	Formatting US zip codes and Canadian postal codes

Here's the app we're building in this workshop session:

We're building a reusable AddressForm component, an Address to use in it, and a Tester app to demonstrate switching between Addresses and show how the AddressForm correctly responds. (Like all the code in this book, the AddressForm is MIT-licensed, so you can use it in your own commercial apps.)

As shown in the following screen, when you click an Address in the top List, you populate the AddressForm with the Address you selected.

I'll show screenshots of how this app behaves as we go into code; for now, let's start by looking at the Tester app.

session26/src/Tester.mxml

```
<?xml version="1.0" encoding="utf-8"?>
<s:Application
  xmlns:fx="http://ns.adobe.com/mxml/2009"
  xmlns:s="library://ns.adobe.com/flex/spark"
  xmlns:mx="library://ns.adobe.com/flex/halo"
  xmlns:comp="components.*"
  width="100%" height="100%">
<fx:Script><![CDATA[
  import mx.controls.Alert;
  import mx.collections.ArrayCollection;
  import model.Address;

  [Bindable]
  private var _addresses:ArrayCollection = new ArrayCollection([    ❶
    new Address("1944 S El Camino Real", "", "San Mateo",
      "CA", "USA", "94403"),
    new Address("788 Denman Street", "", "Vancouver",
      "BC", "Canada", "V6G 2L5"),
    new Address("25 Oxford Street", "", "London",
      "", "UK", "W1D 2DW"),
    new Address("21 Water Street", "#400", "Vancouver",
      "BC", "Canada", "V6B 1A1")]);

  protected function submitClickHandler(event:MouseEvent):void {    ❷
    if (addressForm.validateAndSave()) {
      Alert.show("I can haz credit card next?", "Address Valid!");
```

```
    } else {
      Alert.show("I haz errors", "Oh Noes!");
    }
  }

  private function enterNewAddress():void {
    addressList.selectedItem = null;
  }
]]></fx:Script>
  <s:layout>
    <s:VerticalLayout paddingLeft="10" paddingTop="10" gap="5"/>
  </s:layout>
  <s:List id="addressList" dataProvider="{_addresses}"
    width="380" height="60"/>
  <s:Button label="Enter New Address" click="enterNewAddress()"/
  >
  <s:Panel title="Address">
    <s:layout>
      <s:VerticalLayout paddingLeft="5" paddingTop="5" gap="10"/>
    </s:layout>
    <comp:AddressForm id="addressForm"
      address="{addressList.selectedItem}"/>
  </s:Panel>
  <s:Button label="Submit" click="submitClickHandler(event)"/>
</s:Application>
```

❸
❹
❺
❻

❶ The _addresses ArrayCollection of test Addresses holds the addresses we'll use. (The first two are of Santa Ramen and Kintaro Ramen, both of which I love.)

❷ The submitClickHandler function validates and saves the Address and shows an alert based on the result.

❸ The enterNewAddress function simply sets the selectedItem to null, which also triggers the binding to the address property.

❹ The addressList has a dataProvider of _addresses.

❺ The AddressForm has its address property bound to the selectedItem of the addressList.

❻ The Submit button click event triggers the submitClickHandler.

We start by creating an ArrayCollection ❶ of _addresses, which is used as the dataProvider of the addressList ❹. The selectedItem of this List is passed into the AddressForm ❺ that we're building. We have a Submit button ❻ whose click event is handled by a function that calls the validateAndSave ❷ method of the AddressForm and shows one of two Alert messages based on the outcome. We can also click an Enter New Address button that calls the enterNewAddress() function ❸ to null out the existing address.

The following figure shows an Alert that happens on a validation error.

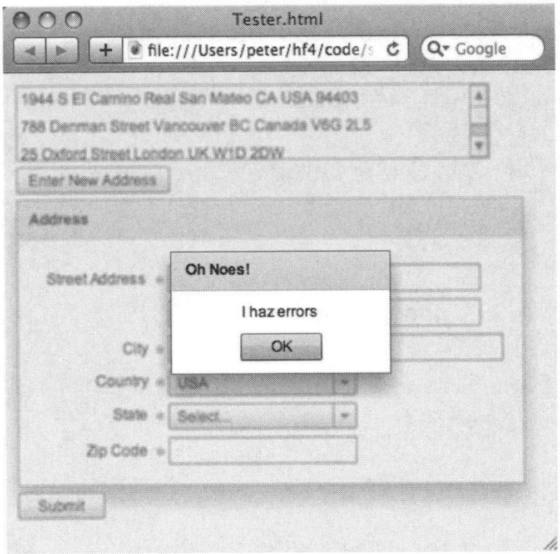

Similarly, here's what happens when all the validations succeed:

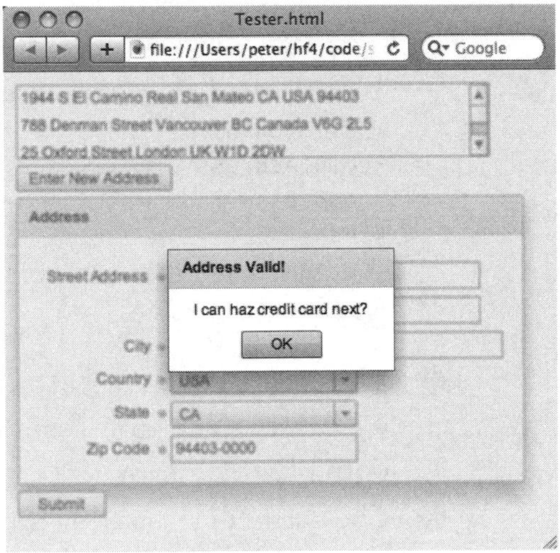

Next, we create the Address model class.

session26/src/model/Address.as

```
package model {
  [Bindable]
  public class Address {
    public var lineOne:String;
    public var lineTwo:String;
    public var city:String;
    public var zipCode:String;
    public var state:String;
    public var country:String;
```

❶

```
public function Address(                              ◄──┐
  lineOne:String = "",                                   ❷
  lineTwo:String = "",
  city:String = "",
  state:String = "",
  country:String = "",
  zipCode:String = "") {
  this.lineOne = lineOne;
  this.lineTwo = lineTwo;
  this.city = city;
  this.state = state;
  this.country = country;
  this.zipCode = zipCode;
}

private function getAddrStr(str:String):String {
  return (str == null || str == "") ? "" : str + " ";
]

public function toString():String {                   ◄──┐
  return getAddrStr(lineOne) + getAddrStr(lineTwo) +     ❸
    getAddrStr(city) + getAddrStr(state) +
    getAddrStr(country) + getAddrStr(zipCode);
  }
 }
}
```

The Address model is pretty straightforward: we want every variable to be bindable, so we stick a [Bindable] annotation ❶ on the class. (Making things bindable results in more code being generated, so don't abuse this notation.) Second, we create a constructor ❷ that has default values (the empty string) for all its parameters. This lets us just specify some (or none) of the parameters when creating a new Address. Finally, we create a toString function ❸ which uses a getAddrStr utility method to ensure that Addresses with only some fields specified don't have a bunch of extra spaces. (Yes, it will have one extra space at the end; fixing this is an exercise for the reader.)

Just as in Java, the toString method is called whenever an object needs to be presented as a String form, and it's often overridden to present the information in a more usable manner. Note that what I'm doing here is OK in the `toString` method, but in general the model code should not define view level information.

Before we create the `AddressForm`, I'm going to show a number of screenshots that demonstrate the various features of the `AddressForm`, and that show how it performs with validation errors.

First, the following screenshot shows that when a US zip code is entered for a Canadian postal code, a proper validation message is displayed. (This is something that currently doesn't happen out of the box with the `ZipCodeValidator`, and it's one of the things we're fixing in this example.)

Also note that the form labels say "Province" and "Postal Code," not "State" and "Zip Code," when the country is Canada.

Next, note that when a Canadian postal code is entered for a US zip code, the validation error is displayed and the erroneous text isn't cleared out by the formatter.

Once you're done coding this example, you'll be able to see the formatters in action, updating the zip codes to the 5+4 modern US style, and uppercasing Canadian postal codes and adding a space in them.

Yes, it's as thrilling as it sounds.

Finally, the following screenshot shows that we're also using a validator to require that a state be chosen for the USA (or a province for Canada), and also requiring a zip code/postal code for the USA or Canada.

For countries that aren't the USA or Canada, we don't require a province or postal code, as this screenshot shows:

Not only are there no validation errors, but there are no red asterisks on the form indicating that the province or postal code is required.

Without further ado, let's create the AddressForm. (Finally!) This is a lot of code, so we'll take a few breaks along the way and explain what we're doing.

session26/src/components/AddressForm.mxml

```
<?xml version="1.0" encoding="utf-8"?>
<mx:Form
  xmlns:fx="http://ns.adobe.com/mxml/2009"
  xmlns:s="library://ns.adobe.com/flex/spark"
  xmlns:mx="library://ns.adobe.com/flex/halo"
  width="400">
<fx:Script><![CDATA[
  import mx.collections.ArrayCollection;
  import mx.events.ValidationResultEvent;
  import mx.validators.Validator;
  import model.Address;

  private var _address:Address = new Address();               ❶

  public function validateAndSave():Boolean {                 ❷
    if (isFormValid()) {
      address.lineOne = addressOneTI.text;
      address.lineTwo = addressTwoTI.text;
      address.city = cityTI.text;
      address.country = countryDDL.selectedItem;
      if (stateDDL.dataProvider.length == 0) {
        address.state = "";
      } else {
        address.state = stateDDL.selectedItem;                ❸
      }
      address.zipCode = zipTI.text;
      return true;
    } else {
      return false;
    }
  }
  private function isFormValid():Boolean {                     ❹
    var validators:Array = [addressValidator, cityValidator,
```

```
        countryValidator, stateValidator];
    var zipCodeValid:Boolean = validateAndFormatZipCode();
    var results:Array = Validator.validateAll(validators);
    return results.length == 0 && zipCodeValid;
}
private function setFormFromAddress():void {
    addressOneTI.text = address.lineOne;
    addressTwoTI.text = address.lineTwo;
    cityTI.text = address.city;
    countryDDL.selectedItem = address.country;
    var states:ArrayCollection = getStates(address.country);
    stateDDL.dataProvider = states;
    stateDDL.selectedIndex = states.source.indexOf(address.state);
    zipTI.text = address.zipCode;
}
...
```

❺

❶ The _address holds the Address this AddressForm is editing.

❷ The validateAndSave method is called by the Tester app. It calls isFormValid to check whether the form components are all valid, and if so, it updates the address with the state of the form components. This approach is used to ensure that we don't corrupt the Address with invalid or only partially valid data.

❸ We assign "" for the state when the selectedItem is null (for when there is no selected item), such as when the states/provinces list is empty for a given country.

❹ The isFormValid method runs the validators by constructing an array of them and calling Validator.validateAll with this Array. It also runs the zip code validator separately by calling a function called validateAndFormatZipCode, which we'll see later. If there are any validation errors in the Validator.validateAll call, the results.length will be nonzero. Note that we use a temporary variable for zipCodeValid since we don't want the validation to short-circuit and not call the validateAndFormatZipCode method. (Our intention is to call all the validators to show all the validation errors at once.)

❺ The setFormFromAddress method updates the state of the form from the state of the address. Because this is all done inside one method, we can be sure that we have set the country correctly before updating the states. When you see the following form code, the importance of this will become clearer.

session26/src/components/AddressForm.mxml (continued)

```
...
public function set address(value:Address):void {
  if (value == null) {
    _address = new Address();
    setFormFromAddress();
  } else {
    _address = value;
    setFormFromAddress();
    callLater(isFormValid);
  }
}
[Bindable]
public function get address():Address {
  return _address;
}

private static const EMPTY:ArrayCollection =
  new ArrayCollection([]);
private static const COUNTRIES:ArrayCollection =
  new ArrayCollection(["USA", "Canada", "UK", "France"]);
private static const STATES:ArrayCollection =
  new ArrayCollection(["CA", "OR", "WA"]);
private static const PROVINCES:ArrayCollection =
  new ArrayCollection(["BC", "AB", "SK"]);

private function getStates(country:String):ArrayCollection {
  if (isUSA(country)) {
    return STATES;
  } else if (isCanada(country)) {
    return PROVINCES;
  } else {
    return EMPTY;
  }
}
private function usaOrCanada(country:String):Boolean {
  return isUSA(country) || isCanada(country);
```

6

7

8

9

```
}
private function isUSA(country:String):Boolean {
  return country == "USA";
}
private function isCanada(country:String):Boolean {
  return country == "Canada";
}
private function getStateMsg(country:String):String {
  return isUSA(country) ? "Please choose a state." :
    "Please choose a province.";
}
...
```

6 The address setter creates a new `Address` if the passed-in value is `null`. In both cases, the `setFormFromAddress` function is called after this address is set. However, when there is a non-`null` value passed in, we also invoke the `isFormValid` method (shown earlier) by using the `callLater` method. By using `callLater`, we ensure that the form controls have had time to reflect the new values that they have been set to. (I haven't talked about `callLater` in this book since it's an advanced technique. Basically, it runs a function later—that is, in the next screen refresh—so that values have had the chance to get set.) The reason that we only run the validation when setting a non-`null` `Address` is that we don't want an empty form to show a bunch of validation errors—that would look ugly. (Also, since the user hasn't made any mistakes—yet—on an empty form, it would be misleading!) Below this method, we also create an address getter which is much simpler.

7 These constants are obviously "book code." Yes, there are more countries in the world, and more states and provinces than I've shown. I just saved a tree.

8 The `getStates` function returns `STATES` for the USA, `PROVINCES` for Canada, and `EMPTY` for the rest of the world. This is the North America–centric behavior we want; "international" readers can feel free to modify this code as necessary!

9 These four convenience functions are used in the form to show/hide required asterisks beside the children of the `FormItems`. I created them since I use them in bindings, and they read nicely.

session26/src/components/AddressForm.mxml (continued)

```
...
  private function validateAndFormatZipCode():Boolean {
    var unformattedText:String =
      zipTI.text.toUpperCase().replace(/\W/g, "");
    var country:String = countryDDL.selectedItem;
    var result:ValidationResultEvent;
    var usa:Boolean = isUSA(country);
    var canada:Boolean = isCanada(country);
    zipCodeValidator.required = usa;
    postalCodeValidator.required = canada;
    if (usa) {
      postalCodeValidator.validate("");
      result = zipCodeValidator.validate(unformattedText);
    } else if (canada) {
      zipCodeValidator.validate("");
      result = postalCodeValidator.validate(unformattedText);
    } else {
      postalCodeValidator.validate("");
      zipCodeValidator.validate("");
      return true;
    }
    if (result.type == ValidationResultEvent.VALID) {
      if (usa) {
        zipTI.text = zipCodeFormatter.format(unformattedText);
      } else {
        zipTI.text = postalCodeFormatter.format(unformattedText);
      }
      return true;
    } else {
      return false;
    }
  }
}
]]></fx:Script>
  <fx:Declarations>
    <mx:StringValidator id="addressValidator" minLength="5"
      source="{addressOneTI}" property="text" required="true"/>
    <mx:StringValidator id="cityValidator" minLength="2"
      source="{cityTI}" property="text" required="true"/>
    <mx:NumberValidator id="countryValidator"
      lowerThanMinError="Please choose a country."
      source="{countryDDL}" property="selectedIndex" minValue="0"/>
    <mx:NumberValidator id="stateValidator"
```

⑩ ⑪ ⑫ ⑬ ⑭ ⑮

```
    lowerThanMinError="{getStateMsg(countryDDL.selectedItem)}"
    source="{stateDDL}" property="selectedIndex"
    enabled="{usaOrCanada(countryDDL.selectedItem)}"          ⟵
    minValue="0"/>                                              ⓰
  <mx:ZipCodeFormatter id="zipCodeFormatter"          ⟵
    formatString="#####-####"/>                        ⓱
  <mx:ZipCodeFormatter id="postalCodeFormatter"               ⟵
    formatString="### ###"/>                                    ⓲
  <mx:ZipCodeValidator id="zipCodeValidator"          ⟵
    listener="{zipTI}"/>                               ⓳
  <mx:RegExpValidator id="postalCodeValidator"  ⟵
    listener="{zipTI}"                           ⓴
    expression="^[A-Z]\d[A-Z]\d[A-Z]\d$"
    noMatchError="The postal code is invalid."/>
</fx:Declarations>
...
```

⓾ The `validateAndFormatZipCode` function returns whether the zip or postal code was valid and successfully formatted.

⑪ For the USA, the `zipCodeValidator` is run.

⑫ For Canada, the `postalCodeValidator` is run.

⑬ If the result is `VALID`, the formatters are run. The `zipCodeFormatter` is run for the USA; the `postalCodeFormatter` is run for Canada. (Since only the USA and Canada get their zip/postal codes validated, the else case is legitimate.)

⑭ We create `StringValidator` instances that ensure that the input meets a certain minimum length. The source object is the component that contains the `property` that is being validated.

⑮ The `countryValidator` and `stateValidator` are `NumberValidator` instances, which are run on the `selectedIndex` properties of the `DropDownList`s for the country and state. Yes, this is considered the best practice.

⑯ The `stateValidator` is only enabled for the USA or Canada.

⑰ The `zipCodeFormatter` uses US zip code 5+4 format.

⑱ The `postalCodeFormatter` is, confusingly enough, a `ZipCodeFormatter`.

⑲ The `zipCodeValidator` uses the built-in `ZipCodeValidator`.

⑳ The `postalCodeValidator` uses the built-in `RegExpValidator` to validate Canadian postal codes using regular expressions.

session26/src/components/AddressForm.mxml (continued)

```
...
  <mx:FormItem label="Street Address" required="true" width="100%">    ㉑
    <s:TextInput id="addressOneTI" width="250"/>
    <s:TextInput id="addressTwoTI" width="250"/>
  </mx:FormItem>
  <mx:FormItem label="City" required="true" width="100%">
    <s:TextInput id="cityTI" width="100%"/>
  </mx:FormItem>
  <mx:FormItem label="Country" required="true">                        ㉒
    <s:DropDownList id="countryDDL" width="150"
      dataProvider="{COUNTRIES}" prompt="Select..."
      change="validateAndFormatZipCode();"/>
  </mx:FormItem>
  <mx:FormItem                                                         ㉓
    label="{isUSA(countryDDL.selectedItem) ? 'State' : 'Province'}"
    required="{usaOrCanada(countryDDL.selectedItem)}">
    <s:DropDownList id="stateDDL" width="150"
      dataProvider="{getStates(countryDDL.selectedItem)}"             ㉔
      prompt="Select..."
      enabled="{stateDDL.dataProvider.length > 0}"/>
  </mx:FormItem>
  <mx:FormItem                                                         ㉕
    label="{isUSA(countryDDL.selectedItem) ? 'Zip' : 'Postal'} Code"
    width="100%" required="{usaOrCanada(countryDDL.selectedItem)}">
    <s:TextInput id="zipTI" width="150"
      focusOut="validateAndFormatZipCode()"/>                         ㉖
  </mx:FormItem>
</mx:Form>
```

㉑ The `FormItem` components are just layout tools, much like the `Form` itself is. There is no special functionality in the `Form` container: unlike HTML Forms, a Flex Halo `Form` is *just a layout tool*.

㉒ The countries are in a `countryDDL` `DropDownList`. When the country changes, we call `validateAndFormatZipCode()` to ensure the zip/postal code validation is current.

㉓ The `selectedItem` of the `countryDDL` is used to determine whether the `FormItems` are required. All that this property on the `FormItem` means is that a little red asterisk is displayed. It has *no* effect on the controls inside the `FormItem` unless those controls also use it.

㉔ The `dataProvider` of the `stateDDL` is determined by the `selectedItem` of the `countryDDL`.

㉕ The `selectedItem` of the `countryDDL` is used to determine the label of the `FormItem` for zip/postal code and state/province.

㉖ The `zipTI` `focusOut` event triggers the `validateAndFormatZipCode` function, to ensure that errors in zip and postal codes are caught right away.

Phew!

That was a very long example, and it even involved a bit of regular expressions. Sorry about that—if I'd told you up front that was what

I USED TO CODE REGULAR EXPRESSIONS UPHILL, BOTH WAYS. IN PERL.

you were in for, you may have skipped it! Thankfully, Flex has a `RegExpValidator` that lets us construct a regular expression-using validator very easily.

Who knew zip codes and postal codes could be so complicated? (Furthermore, we've totally ignored the rest of the world—so doing this properly would be much worse!)

➤ Key points

○ Flex comes with a number of useful formatters and validators.

○ Flex makes it (relatively) easy to build custom components that use both formatters and validators to be as user-friendly as possible.

○ Be careful of using data binding in form components that are interdependent, such as country and state `DropDownList` components. You could create a form that works well when modifying a new model object, but that doesn't handle the model object being set from the outside world properly.

○ In some situations, `callLater` can be used to work around tricky UI timing issues. However, it's something that should be used

LUXURY! I CODED REGULAR EXPRESSIONS IN BINARY, USING PUNCH CARDS.

carefully, as it's prone to being abused and not solving the underlying problems.

○ `Form` and `FormItem` are *just layout tools*. There's no need to use them to submit forms, unlike what you do in HTML. Think of them as a `VGroup` customized to display forms nicely.

What's next?

VERY CUTE SID. BUT WHY IS IT THAT WHENEVER YOU GUYS TALK ABOUT REGULAR EXPRESSIONS OR ANYTHING TECHNICAL DOES IT REALLY HAVE TO TURN INTO A ... CONTEST?

As we have seen throughout the book, Flex makes it easy to create custom components. In this session we've gone deep into formatters and validators, creating a custom validator and a complex custom form component.

I don't know about you, but—despite their usefulness—I'm getting sick of forms. In the next chapter we'll do something completely different and have some fun, as we finally build our Twitter + Yahoo! Maps mashup. This will demonstrate how real-world Flex applications are built, how to architect larger Flex applications using Cairngorm, and how to talk to servers using `HTTPService`.

7

Cairngorm in Action:
SocialStalkr
(Twitter + Yahoo! Maps)

I n this chapter, you'll learn how to build larger Flex applications using a framework called Cairngorm. This is a topic that can only be learned by experience, and it's best done iteratively. Doing so properly, though, would consume over a hundred pages: in early versions of this book I built this example iteratively over five chapters, explaining Flex as I went. But this approach didn't fit

with the format of the "Hello" series, so I rewrote the book and added the stand-alone examples instead. So, since this chapter covers

what used to be explained in five chapters, it will be very code heavy. Instead of building it iteratively, I'm going to show the screenshots of the app, explain the design choices, and then present the end result—explaining the code as I go.

This chapter covers the following topics:

◉ Using Cairngorm to structure Flex applications

◉ Separating a Flex application into multiple components

◉ Using HTTPService to talk to RESTful web services,[1] specifically the Twitter API

◉ Using the Yahoo! Maps API

As you can see, it's an ambitious chapter. By the end of it you'll have a much better handle on how to build real-world Flex applications, not just apps that are the size of the toy examples we've been building so far in this book.

So, let's get started.

Creating the SocialStalkr project

The application we are going to build in this chapter is called SocialStalkr: a mashup of Yahoo! Maps and Twitter that lets you "stalk" your friends who use specially formatted   Twitter "tweets"   on   a

---

[1]   REST (Representational State Transfer) is a way of building web services that focuses on simplicity and an architecture style that is "of the web." This can be described as a resource-oriented architecture (ROA); see *RESTful Web Services* (O'Reilly 2007) for details. As you can probably infer from its $20-word full title, REST grew out of a PhD thesis—Roy Fielding's, to be precise. However, unlike most PhD theses, it has grown into something revolutionary.

Yahoo! map. At the end of this chapter, the app will have the following screenshots:

First, when the app starts, a login screen appears. You'll log in with your Twitter credentials, and then see the main app. The left side of the app shows a Yahoo! map; in the right side the "You" view shows your tweets (and lets you post new tweets).

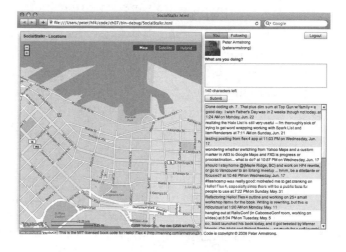

Also, in the right side, you can switch from the "You" view to the "Following" view, which shows your friends, who you can select to view their tweets. As shown in the figure showing the Following view, the itemRenderer grows larger and shows for the selected friend the web-standard "followed link" purple color, and for the friend you're mousing over the web-standard "click this link" blue link color.

So we're building a Twitter client. But why is there a map anyway, and what does this app have to do with "stalking" your friends? And why would your friends want you to do this?

Well, for example, regular users of Twitter often use @replies to people and #hashtags. Sometimes, people also say that they're going to #somewhere to do something, for example "off to #ChillWinston for a pint." So, if we took this one step further and got people to adopt some conventions (which, if we were being pretentious, we could call a "microformat"), they could use Twitter and SocialStalkr to become a location-aware and time-sensitive spontaneous event planner.

For example, the following screen shows me tweeting that I just spent some time at WorkSpace in Vancouver working on this chapter of the book. Say Scott Patten, my partner in Ruboss, saw that tweet—if he was downtown he could come visit me and we could go for a pint. Or, if you were a friend who didn't know where WorkSpace was, my tweet would be showing right there on top of its location on the map, as shown in the figure.

Finally, a cynical reason: microblogging services such as Twitter are an exercise in narcissism as much as an attempt at real communication, so what better Twitter client than one that sticks your own avatar all over a map?

Yeah, it's a bit contrived. But it will be fun to build—and there are many location-based social network startups that are doing a similar thing (but with automatic location detection based on your smartphone). So, you can imagine taking this app further and making it useful. Furthermore, since I'm not using any server-side technology in this book (this isn't a book about Java, Ruby on Rails, or ColdFusion after all), I'm basically limited to mashups of existing web services for examples.

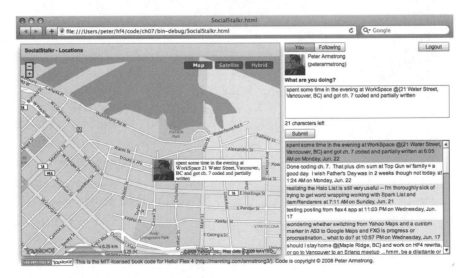

So, now that we have the requirements and visual design out of the way, let's create the project. In Flash Builder 4, choose File > New > Flex Project to trigger the New Flex Project dialog. Enter the name **SocialStalkr** for the project in the Project Name field and click Finish.

TIP   If you name a project in the same case as what you want your main application to be— that is, SocialStalkr instead of socialstalkr—you can skip the rest of the New Project dialog and you won't need to rename the application. It's good practice to CamelCase your application name: since it's a class like any other class in your app, it would be confusing to be called socialstalkr since it would look like a variable and not a class.

With this accomplished, let's get started with Twitter and Yahoo! Maps.

Getting started with Twitter

If you don't already have a Twitter account, you need to go to www.twitter.com and create one. This way, you can enter specially formatted tweets that will show up on the Yahoo! map we'll be integrating later in this chapter. When you sign up with Twitter, you'll get a unique login ID and a unique screen name; for example, my screen name is peterarmstrong so on Twitter I'm http://twitter.com/peterarmstrong.

Web services can be unreliable

Before we continue, a cautionary note: at any time during the process of following along with this book, your application may stop working for no apparent reason. This is always a danger when working with web services, but with Twitter it has historically been, shall we say, more of a danger than normal. If this happens, try running the app in the debugger. If you see something like the following, chances are it's Twitter's fault:

[RPC Fault faultString="HTTP request error" faultCode="Server.Error.Request" faultDetail="Error: [IOErrorEvent type="ioError" bubbles=false cancelable=false eventPhase=2 text="Error #2032: Stream Error. URL: http://twitter.com/statuses/friends/peterarmstrong.xml"]. URL: http://twitter.com/statuses/friends/peterarmstrong.xml"]

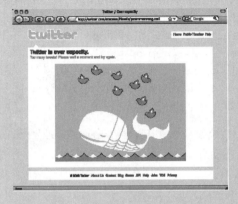

If you see this, try checking your friends' statuses by going to http://twitter.com/statuses/friends/YOUR_SCREEN_NAME.xml (for example, I go to http://twitter.com/statuses/friends/peterarmstrong.xml). If you can see your friends' statuses via XML, then Twitter is fine and you should try your app again. However, if you see the image of the now infamous Twitter "Fail Whale,"[a] you should just go grab a coffee and come back and try again. (Twitter's reliability has gotten a lot better in 2009 than it was in 2008, so this hopefully shouldn't be a problem. However, the scaling problems they had in 2008 were the comedy gift that kept on giving: my favorite mean-spirited TechCrunch headline of all time was "Twitter Suffers Minor Period of Uptime."[b])

a. http://en.wikipedia.org/wiki/Fail_Whale
b. www.techcrunch.com/2008/06/06/twitter-suffers-minor-period-of-uptime-overnight/

TIP Another reason your service can fail is that you may have exceeded your API quota, which is something like 100 requests per hour. So, if you do lot of debugging involving clicking on your friends to view their tweets, you may need to take a forced coffee break every so often.

Anyway, with this out of the way, we're almost ready to talk to Twitter. First, let's make sure that you have some data to play with. Post some "tweets" (messages that are fewer than 140 characters) and "follow" some people. You don't have to know them, but it's more interesting if you do. If you have no friends on Twitter, you can always follow me (@peterarmstrong) and my Ruboss partner Scott Patten (scott_patten)—the app we are building in this chapter is more interesting with at least two friends. (Note that I'm saying "friends" even though the following relationship is unidirectional, unlike the bidirectional "friend" relationship on services like Facebook. This is just because the phrase "people the user is following" is a mouthful.)

Now that we're ready to talk to Twitter, we need to get ready to talk to Yahoo! Maps.

Getting started with Yahoo! Maps

Next, we'll sign up for Yahoo! to use Yahoo! Maps. Why would I choose Yahoo! instead of Google? There's a practical reason: at the time of this writing, the terms of service for Yahoo! Maps were nicer. (Also, Ryan Stewart has posted an excellent blog post[2] on how to use FXG assets and the ActionScript API with Google Maps, so there's no need to duplicate his work.)

Let's start by signing up for the Yahoo! Developer Network at http://developer.yahoo. com. You'll need to get a Yahoo! ID if you don't already have one. Next, go to http:// developer.yahoo.com/ maps/ and click the Get an App ID button on the page to get an application ID. You'll see a screen like the following. Enter information specific to you and your own organization, but leave the "Generic, No user authentication required" setting chosen so that the example in this chapter works.

(Since URLs change, if that URL doesn't work, go to http://developer.yahoo.com/wsregapp or just http://developer.yahoo.com/ and follow your nose.)

Click Continue. You'll see something like this:

Copy this application ID and save it into a text file somewhere—you'll need to paste it into your Flex code. (The "application entrypoint" is unimportant for our purposes, so we're ignoring it.)

YAHOO! MAPS DOCUMENTATION

This book is certainly not trying to be a comprehensive Yahoo! Maps tutorial; it's just an example that we're using. The Yahoo! Developer Network page for the maps component (http://developer.yahoo.com/flash/maps/examples.html) as well as the API documentation (http://developer.yahoo.com/flash/maps/classreference/index.html) are the best places to start learning more about Yahoo! Maps.

Now that we have an application ID, we can download the Yahoo! Maps AS3 Component from http://developer.yahoo.com/flash/maps/. This book is using version 0.9.3 of this component; chances are you'll use a newer version. (If a newer version doesn't work for you, just grab the version I used from the code zip file for the book.) Once you've downloaded it, you'll have a file like yahoo-maps-as3-api-0.9.3-beta.zip saved somewhere. Unzip it and copy the YahooMap.swc file from the Build/Flex directory into your libs directory of SocialStalkr. SWC files are compiled libraries, and any SWC files you put in your libs directory in a Flex project are automatically included when compiling.

Now that we've signed up for Twitter and gotten set up with Yahoo!, we can get down to work. First, we need to learn how to architect our application. While there are many newer application frameworks like Swiz, Mate, and PureMVC that have very vocal adherents, we'll use

Cairngorm. Cairngorm is currently the de facto standard application framework for Flex, and it's not clear which of the challengers will emerge as the best alternative. So, I'm going to teach the standard. Whether or not you'll use it, every Flex developer needs to know Cairngorm—if only to understand what the other frameworks are reacting to.

Cairngorm

We're building the SocialStalkr application using Cairngorm. However, we'll use Cairngorm in a slightly nonstandard way, in order to be slightly less verbose and to make the use of HTTPService easier. Specifically, we'll use a couple of utility classes from my *Flexible Rails* book (Manning, 2008) to this effect. (These classes have nothing to do with Ruby on Rails; they're just focused on making Cairngorm + HTTPService less verbose.)

Since Cairngorm has so many moving parts that work together, it's very difficult to build this example iteratively—and as discussed at the beginning of the chapter, it would take too long. So, I'm just going to explain the finished result. As you see more and more of the code, you'll grasp how it all fits together—so don't worry if *why* we're doing something isn't 100 percent apparent at the time. By the end of the chapter, it will be.

Above all, keep in mind that Cairngorm is a Model-View-Controller (MVC) framework. As we create the various files, think about where they fit in the MVC pattern.

WOW, HE'S GETTING SELF-PROMOTIONAL NOW! MAYBE HE THINKS HE IS 37SIGNALS?

> *Flexible Rails*, **Cairngorm, and this book**
> The way that Cairngorm is used is based on section 8.1 of my *Flexible Rails* book. Even though we aren't using Ruby on Rails in this book, the way that Flex uses HTTPService is essentially the same regardless of what is on the server side. So, since I already spent a whole book writing about how Flex should talk to Rails, it would be dishonest of me to pretend *Flexible Rails* didn't exist and to ignore the approaches I used in it. Because of this, I'm feeling free to borrow a couple of utility classes from *Flexible Rails* for this section—and, while I'm at it, to make this section of this chapter a condensed version of sections 8.1 and 8.2 of *Flexible Rails*. If you *have* already read *Flexible Rails*, please feel free to skim until you get to the code.

Cairngorm history and motivation

One of the biggest problems with Flex is that it makes writing code almost too easy. How can this be a problem? Well, as we've seen, it's possible to get a *lot* done without giving any thought to your application's design. This can be dangerous: if other people (such as your client or marketing department) see a prototype running, they may get confused into thinking you have a fully functional app instead of an elaborate mock-up. Another problem is that if we develop iteratively without any refactoring *(or thinking)*, we can end up with Rube Goldberg–like contraptions in our MXML:

> *...this variable gets set, which triggers this binding, which updates this model element, which in turn updates this model element, which triggers this function, which dispatches this event, which...*

Because Flex is so easy, it's possible to have somewhat working code even with a terrible muddle. All the Flex application frameworks try to solve this problem; as discussed, Cairngorm is what we're going to pick for this chapter.

Cairngorm was created by Steven Webster and Alistair McLeod, the two cofounders of a consulting firm called iteration::two, which was based in Scotland. They were acquired by Macromedia, which was then acquired by Adobe. (Steven and Alistair are famous in Flex circles for having written the definitive book on Flex 1.0, *Developing Rich Clients with Macromedia Flex*.) Cairngorm embodies many of Steven's and McLeod's opinions about how to write Flex applications. Because their book helped many developers (myself included) to learn Flex, these opinions have a lot of clout. And because Steven and Alistair are now at Adobe (and Cairngorm is at Adobe Labs), Cairngorm has gained even more mindshare among Flex developers because of its somewhat "official" status.

That said, you certainly don't need to use Cairngorm. Steven Webster wrote a blog post titled "Why I think you shouldn't use Cairngorm," (http://blogs.adobe.com/swebster/archives/2006/08/why_i_think_you.html), which lists some prerequisites for using Cairngorm. Essentially, Cairngorm can be overkill for small, single-developer applications (such as this one), and it can be confusing if you've never built a complete Flex application before. (We're up for the challenge, though—we're not "dummies" after all.) If, at the end of this chapter, you decide that you don't like Cairngorm, don't worry: you can develop complete, innovative Flex applications without using Cairngorm. For example, I currently spend most of my time developing Flex applications using RestfulX. (Of course, the RestfulX framework was formerly known as the Ruboss Framework, so I'm more than a little biased here.)

If you want to learn more about Cairngorm, the site www.cairngorm-docs.org/ is devoted to collecting links to Cairngorm documentation and examples. In terms of tutorial documentation, the best starting place is the six-part article series that Steven Webster wrote for the Flex Developer Center. Part 1 is at www.adobe.com/devnet/flex/articles/cairngorm_pt1_print.html, and each part links to the next one. The articles develop an application called CairngormStore, which is a simple online store. These articles are rather outdated: at the time of this writing, Cairngorm is at version 2.2.1; the articles refer to version 0.99. However, they're a good way to learn the theory of Cairngorm, even if many of the details have changed.

I'm going to assume that if you're interested in using Cairngorm, you've read these articles or will read them; as such, I won't duplicate their content. This book won't include a 5–10 page "theory of Cairngorm" section. Instead, we'll learn Cairngorm by doing, building the Social-Stalkr application from scratch using Cairngorm 2.2.1. If at the end of this chapter you want to look through more Cairngorm-using code, take a look at the updated version of Chen Bekor's ModifiedCairngormStore at www.brightworks.com/flex_ability/?p=61.

Downloading and installing Cairngorm 2.2.1

We'll start by downloading Cairngorm 2.2.1. It's currently found at http://opensource.adobe.com/wiki/display/cairngorm/Downloads. Download the binary, source, and documentation zip files from the three separate links.

NOTE   Download Cairngorm 2.2.1, not Cairngorm Enterprise 2.2.1. (Cairngorm Enterprise is for LiveCycle Data Services.)

Unzip these files into their own folders. Next, we'll import the Cairngorm project into Flex Builder so that we can easily browse it. (The zip file includes a Flex Builder .project file.) In Flex Builder, choose File > Import > Other. Choose Existing Projects into Workspace, and click Next. In the Import dialog, browse to the Cairngorm2_2_1-src directory that was created when we unzipped the Cairngorm 2.2.1 sources. You'll know you found it when you see the Cairngorm project highlighted in the Projects list. Click Finish to import the project. Once the project is imported, you can browse the source code, starting by expanding the com folder.

There isn't much code in Cairngorm, so you should read it all at some point.

Now that we've downloaded Cairngorm, let's add it to SocialStalkr. Copy the Cairngorm.swc file from the Cairngorm 2.2.1 binary download into the libs directory of the SocialStalkr project. (This is the same directory that we put the YahooMap.swc library into in chapter 2.)

That's it; Cairngorm is now usable in SocialStalkr.

Before continuing, the last setup task we'll do is to create *most* of the standard directories that are used in Cairngorm applications. Create an src/com/socialstalkr directory, and inside that directory create the following directories: business, command, control, model and util. (All but the util directory are standard Cairngorm.)

Q. Didn't you forgot the event and vo packages?

A. No, I didn't forget them—I'm omitting them. We aren't going to create custom event subclasses of `CairngormEvent`—instead, we'll go against the officially recommended Cairngorm convention and dispatch plain `CairngormEvents` every time. We'll set the *data* property to an anonymous object containing whatever we need. To me, the reduction in the amount of code is preferable to more type safety (especially on a smaller project such as this). On a larger project with lots of developers, the balance may be different.

Regarding creating a vo package for Value Objects, we're just using XML for now so we don't have any value objects yet. Adding value objects at this point would be packing too much into the refactoring, so we're not going to do it yet.

Cairngorm event sequence overview

Before we begin, I'll present a brief overview of the typical sequence of events in which we'll use Cairngorm. It refers to a bunch of classes we haven't created yet but you should be able to understand what follows. (*If it doesn't make sense now, don't worry*—the goal isn't for it to completely make sense, but for it to make *future sections* make more sense when you read them):

1 A component (for example, the `FollowingGroup` component we'll create for the Twitter users we're following) calls `CairngormUtils.dispatchEvent` with an event type (for example, `EventNames.SHOW_FRIEND_TWEETS`) specified in the `EventNames` class (which is a bunch of `String` constants).

2 Because of the `SocialStalkrController` having called `addCommand` with that event type from `EventNames`, a command (for example, `com.social-stalkr.command.ShowFriendTweets`) has its execute method called.

3 This command creates a new *business delegate* (for example, `com.social-stalkr.business.TwitterDelegate`), which contains functions related to a given web service. It passes itself in as the `IResponder` so that when the business delegate is done, the command's result or fault function will be invoked.

4 In typical Cairngorm applications, the business delegate retrieves services from a Services.mxml file and uses them. We don't do this. Instead, our business delegates themselves delegate all their work (a very businesslike thing to do) to the `ServiceUtils.send()` public static method. This method invokes a URL that invokes the appropriate HTTP service. It also attaches the responder to the service call, so that its result or fault handler will be triggered accordingly.

5 When the service call returns, the `result` or `fault` handler of the command is invoked accordingly. It does what it needs to do, such as making a state change in the `SocialStalkrModelLocator`, dispatching another `CairngormEvent` with `CairngormUtils.dispatchEvent`, and so on.

That's about as much explanation up front as is useful. Let's see some code! (The rest of this chapter is full of code, so grab a coffee.)

Creating the main application

THE MAIN APP IS PRETTY SMALL SINCE ITS JUST A COUPLE COMPONENTS AND VIEW STATES.

Now that we have a new Flex project, a Twitter account with some friends and some tweets of our own, and a Yahoo! developer account, the first bit of actual work we'll do is fill in the main SocialStalkr application file that was created for us. Paste the following code (selecting the text in Adobe Reader shouldn't select the cueballs, so you should be fine) into the src/SocialStalkr.mxml file, or grab the code from manning.com/armstrong3:

ch07/src/SocialStalkr.mxml

```
<?xml version="1.0" encoding="utf-8"?>
<s:Application
  xmlns:fx="http://ns.adobe.com/mxml/2009"
  xmlns:s="library://ns.adobe.com/flex/spark"
  xmlns:mx="library://ns.adobe.com/flex/halo"
  xmlns:components="com.socialstalkr.components.*"
  xmlns:control="com.socialstalkr.control.*">
  <fx:Declarations>
    <control:SocialStalkrController id="controller"/>         ◄———  ❶
  </fx:Declarations>
  <s:states>                                          ❷
    <s:State name="login"/>                       ◄——┘
```

```
      <s:State name="main"/>
    </s:states>
    <components:LoginPanel id="loginPanel"
      includeIn="login"
      horizontalCenter="0" verticalCenter="0"/>
    <components:MainApp id="mainApp"
      includeIn="main"
      left="10" right="10" top="10" bottom="10"/>
</s:Application>
```

1 We use the new `Declarations` element in Flex 4 for nonvisual children, in this case the `SocialStalkrController`.

2 We create two states, a login state and a main state, for the SocialStalkr app. The state determines which of the `LoginPanel` or `MainApp` are visible, since both use `includeIn` to only be in one state.

All Cairngorm apps have a `FrontController`. Ours is the `SocialStalkr-Controller`, which we'll see soon. You need to remember to actually instantiate it by putting it in the `fx:Declarations`, or your app won't function properly. (By this, I mean that your events won't work.) Also, note how we use view states and `includeIn` to simulate the way a `ViewStack` would operate: to show only one child component at a time. View states are much more flexible, however.

Creating the ModelLocator

THE ModelLocator IS WHERE THE SHARED STATE IN THE APP GOES. YES, THIS CAN GET LARGE IF YOU'RE NOT CAREFUL.

Next, let's start by creating the `SocialStalkrModelLoca-tor`. A standard Cairngorm application has one `Model-Locator`, which is a "single place where the application state is held."[3] The app will then bind to the variables in this file directly. This will save us from passing around a bunch of variables.

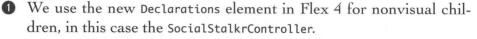

ch07/src/com/socialstalkr/model/SocialStalkrModelLocator.as

```
package com.socialstalkr.model {
  import com.adobe.cairngorm.model.IModelLocator;
```

---

[3] www.adobe.com/devnet/flex/articles/cairngorm_pt2_print.html.

```actionscript
import mx.collections.XMLListCollection;
import mx.formatters.DateFormatter;

                                                                        1
[Bindable]
public class SocialStalkrModelLocator implements IModelLocator {
  private static var _modelLocator:SocialStalkrModelLocator;
  public var userName:String;                                           2
  public var userPassword:String;
  public var twitterUser:XML;
  public var twitterUserTweets:XMLListCollection;
  public var twitterUserFriends:XMLListCollection;
  public var selectedFriend:XML;
  public var selectedFriendTweets:XMLListCollection;
  public var dateFormatter:DateFormatter;
  public var selectedTweet:XML;
                                                                        3
  public function formatTweet(item:Object):String {
    var status:XML = XML(item);
    return status.text + " at " + dateFormatter.format(
      dateFromTwitterDate(status.created_at));
  }                                                                     4

  public static function dateFromTwitterDate(twDate:String):Date {
    return new Date(twDate.substr(0,10) +
        " " + twDate.substr(twDate.length - 4, twDate.length) +
        " " + twDate.substr(11, 8));
  }

  public function SocialStalkrModelLocator(                             5
    enforcer:SingletonEnforcer) {
    dateFormatter = new DateFormatter();
    dateFormatter.formatString = "L:NN A on EEEE, MMM. D";             6
  }

  public static function get instance():                               7
  SocialStalkrModelLocator {
    if (_modelLocator == null) {
      _modelLocator = new SocialStalkrModelLocator(
        new SingletonEnforcer());
    }
    return _modelLocator;
  }
}
```

```
}

class SingletonEnforcer {}
```
← ❽

❶ All variables are `Bindable`.

❷ We implement the `IModelLocator` interface.

❸ The `formatTweet` function formats a tweet using the `dateFormatter` instance variable.

❹ The `dateFromTwitterDate` encapsulates parsing Twitter's date format.

❺ We ensure no other class can construct a `SocialStalkrModelLocator`. (This is explained further below.)

❻ `DateFormatter` lets us easily format dates based on a configurable `formatString`.

❼ This is the getter for a shared instance.

❽ This is the internal `SingletonEnforcer` class..

The `[Bindable]` annotation ❶ on the class means that every public variable is bindable. The public variables in this class represent the shared state in our Flex application. Note that the `SocialStalkrModel-Locator` class implements `com.adobe.cairngorm.model.IModelLocator` ❷. `IModelLocator` is a marker interface: it has no methods. (It does, however, have a comment explaining that classes implementing it should be `Singletons`.) The `SocialStalkrModelLocator` is a `Singleton`, and we accomplish this by making the constructor ❺ take as a parameter an object whose type is `SingletonEnforcer` ❽, which is a private class that's not visible to any other class. (This is a trick I learned from Dima Berastau, creator and lead developer of the RestfulX framework for Flex.) The shared instance is lazily constructed and retrieved with the instance getter ❼. The constructor also sets up the `dateFormatter` ❻.

The `SocialStalkrModelLocator` has all the shared state in the app, as well as some utility functions that use this shared state. The `formatTweet` function formats a tweet ❸, which uses a `dateFromTwitterDate` ❹ function that's heavily based on the `makeDate` function of the `TwitterStatus` class in the Twitterscript API (not covered in this book).

THERE'S AN API? WHY ARE YOU DOING EVERYTHING MANUALLY?

Frankly, I'm doing everything manually since the API is an extremely thin wrapper, and since I'm not trying to teach how to use an API—I'm trying to teach the basics of Flex. If you use the API you never create HTTPServices, for example, and you get a strongly typed object instead of XML. I feel you'll learn more if we just use what's provided by Flex as much as possible. (This won't be true with Yahoo! maps—in that case, we'll use their API.)

If you want to learn more about Twitterscript, see http://code.google.com/p/twitterscript/ for the original version of it. Note that I've forked it on GitHub (www.github.com/peterarmstrong/twitterscript) to make some small fixes to it, and Tony Hillerson has in turn forked my fork to fix authentication with AIR (www.github.com/thillerson/twitterscript). Tony's version will probably be more advanced when you read this, so I recommend looking at both of them.

Creating the control package

Next, we create the control package. It will contain two classes: EventNames and SocialStalkrController.

THIS APPROACH IS STOLEN FROM MY FLEXIBLE RAILS BOOK. REUSE ISN'T JUST FOR SOFTWARE, YOU KNOW…

EventNames.as

First, we create EventNames.as. This isn't a standard Cairngorm class; instead, it's particular to our "no CairngormEvent subclasses" approach.

ch07/src/com/socialstalkr/control/EventNames.as

```
package com.socialstalkr.control {
  public final class EventNames {
    public static const SHOW_USER_TWEETS:String =
      "showUserTweets";
    public static const SHOW_USER_FRIENDS:String =
      "showUserFriends";
    public static const SHOW_FRIEND_TWEETS:String =
      "showFriendTweets";
    public static const POST_TWEET:String = "postTweet";
```

```
    public static const VERIFY_CREDENTIALS:String =
        "verifyCredentials";
   }
}
```

This class lists all the event names, defining constants for each name. This ensures that we won't let a typo give us strange runtime behavior. I prefer this to using Strings everywhere for another reason, too: it makes it easier to check that we aren't using an event name that's already being used.

SAFE AND VERBOSE OR FAST AND LOOSE?

We can pass Strings around without using constants—it's a question of "how much do you hate verbosity?" versus "how much do you value safety?" If we're totally concerned about safety, we create custom events for each event; if we totally hate verbosity, we skip this file. This approach is my compromise.

These event names will be associated with commands, as we'll see next.

SocialStalkrController.as

THE FrontController PATTERN IS A FANCY WAY OF SAYING "LET'S HOOK UP ALL THESE COMMANDS HERE."

After creating the EventNames, we create the Social-StalkrController. This class extends FrontController. A standard Cairngorm application has one FrontController subclass, whose responsibility is to hook up the event names with the commands (which we'll see later). Typically, these event names come from the custom event subclasses; in our case, they come from EventNames.

ch07/src/com/socialstalkr/control/SocialStalkrController.as

```
package com.socialstalkr.control {
    import com.adobe.cairngorm.control.FrontController;
    import com.socialstalkr.control.EventNames
    import com.socialstalkr.command.ShowUserFriends;
    import com.socialstalkr.command.ShowUserTweets;
    import com.socialstalkr.command.ShowFriendTweets;
    import com.socialstalkr.command.PostTweet;
    import com.socialstalkr.command.VerifyCredentials;
```

```
public class SocialStalkrController extends FrontController {    ◁——❶
  public function SocialStalkrController() {
    addCommand(EventNames.SHOW_USER_FRIENDS, ShowUserFriends);    ◁——
    addCommand(EventNames.SHOW_USER_TWEETS, ShowUserTweets);
    addCommand(EventNames.SHOW_FRIEND_TWEETS, ShowFriendTweets);
    addCommand(EventNames.POST_TWEET, PostTweet);
    addCommand(EventNames.VERIFY_CREDENTIALS,                        ❷
      VerifyCredentials);
  }
 }
}
```

We extend `FrontController` ❶ and call the inherited `addCommand` method
❷ for each `EventNames.SOME_NAME_CONSTANT` and command combination.
We'll see the commands soon.

Having created the standard Cairngorm `FrontController` subclass, let's
now add two nonstandard classes to make our lives easier. After this,
we'll go back to adding code that follows the standard Cairngorm patterns.

Creating CairngormUtils and ServiceUtils

Next, we'll add two nonstandard classes from
Flexible Rails that will simplify how we use Cairngorm: `CairngormUtils` and `ServiceUtils`.

THESE TWO CLASSES
ARE LITERALLY TAKEN
VERBATIM. OH WELL,
I LIKED THEM THEN
AND I STILL DO.
OF COURSE, RESTFULX
GOES BEYOND
ServiceUtils.

CairngormUtils.as

First, we'll create the `CairngormUtils` class. Its sole
purpose is to save some typing, since we dispatch
so many events.

ch07/src/com/socialstalkr/util/CairngormUtils.as

```
package com.socialstalkr.util {
  import com.adobe.cairngorm.control.CairngormEvent;
  import com.adobe.cairngorm.control.CairngormEventDispatcher;

  public class CairngormUtils {
    public static function dispatchEvent(
      eventName:String, data:Object = null):void {
```

```
        var event:CairngormEvent = new CairngormEvent(eventName);
        event.data = data;
        event.dispatch();
      }
    }
  }
```

This class defines one public static function, dispatchEvent. It takes a required eventName parameter and an optional data parameter that defaults to null if omitted. It creates a new CairngormEvent with the type set to the eventName. It then sets the untyped data property to the data provided (or null if omitted). Finally, it calls the event's dispatch method, a CairngormEvent method that does the work of getting the shared instance of the CairngormEventDispatcher for us.

ServiceUtils.as

Next, we create a nonstandard class called ServiceUtils, which contains one public static method called send, which we'll use to talk to web services via HTTP. As you'll see, the way that you do this is via a class called HTTPService.

ch07/src/com/socialstalkr/util/ServiceUtils.as

```
package com.socialstalkr.util {
  import mx.rpc.IResponder;
  import mx.rpc.AsyncToken;
  import mx.rpc.http.HTTPService;

  public class ServiceUtils {
    public static function send(                    ←——— ❶
      url:String,                              ←┐
      responder:IResponder = null,              │ ❷
      request:Object = null,
      sendXML:Boolean = false,
      resultFormat:String = "e4x",
      method:String = null,
      useProxy:Boolean = false):void
    {                                                           ❸
      var service:HTTPService = new HTTPService();   ←┘
      service.url = url;
      service.request = request;
```

```
        service.contentType = sendXML ? "application/xml" :           ◄─┐
            "application/x-www-form-urlencoded";                        ❹
        service.resultFormat = resultFormat;
        if (method == null) {
          service.method = (request == null) ? "GET" : "POST";    ◄─┐
        } else {                                                     ❺
          service.method = method;
        }
        service.useProxy = useProxy;                              ❻
        var call:AsyncToken = service.send();              ◄─┘
        if (responder != null) {
          call.addResponder(responder);             ◄─┐
        }                                              ❼
      }
    }
}
```

We create a send function ❶, which has a bunch of parameters. All but the url ❷ parameter have defaults, so only the url parameter (which specifies the URL of the HTTPService) is required. Inside the send function we construct a new HTTPService ❸, set its properties, and call its send ❻ method. The optional parameters specify service properties like the contentType ❹ and method ❺ that have sensible defaults if omitted. The responder is added to the AsyncToken returned by the send() call ❼ so the responder methods can be invoked.

This is the first time in this book that we've seen HTTPService, which is pretty remarkable (and frankly a bit odd) when you think about it—Flex applications are all about talking to servers, and this is the first place we've seen how to do this. However, Flex is a very large topic with lots to cover, as shown by the fact that we could spend most of a book before we got to the point—*talking to one or more servers over HTTP*. The important thing to note about HTTPService is that invoking its send() method ❻ is an *asynchronous* call, so nothing happens immediately in the UI after the send() method is called. (If it was *synchronous*, the UI would block until the call returned.)

INTEGRATING FLEX WITH SERVERS

HTTPService is just one way that Flex applications can talk to servers. Flex can also use WebService and RemoteObject components to talk to servers. In this book, we're sticking with HTTPService, since it's the most flexible: HTTPService lets you integrate with any server-side technology, whether that's Java, PHP, .NET, Ruby on Rails, or whatever. Furthermore, these servers can use "RESTful" APIs to support multiple clients other than Flex, such as HTML and iPhone. If you like RESTful services, I recommend looking into the MIT-licensed RestfulX framework—again, I'm totally biased in favor of RestfulX, however. Finally, a word about HTTPService being asynchronous: Flex programming, when done correctly, involves making a ton of asynchronous service calls and handling their results. Don't try to fight this; just accept that this is fundamental to how Flex code is written and embrace it.

Anyway, back to the ServiceUtils#send() method. You may be wondering why we're doing all this. The answer is that this approach lets us avoid using the standard Cairngorm approach of using a Services.mxml file that defines all the services. That approach is problematic when we use HTTPService a lot, because hardly any properties of a given HTTPService remain constant between service invocations. Worse, if we don't explicitly set the properties to the values we want (even those where we want the default value), we can have unexpected behavior because the properties that a previous use of the HTTPService set will remain set that way. For example, we can have the wrong contentType, resultFormat, and so on if we (or some maintenance programmer) are careless. The disposable HTTPService approach we use here is a lot less bug-prone.

Now that we have the building blocks in place, we can move on to the higher-level classes that use ServiceUtils. First up, since it's next lowest on the food chain, is the TwitterDelegate business delegate. Business delegates are a layer between the low-level plumbing code (in ServiceUtils) and the commands, which we'll describe after the TwitterDelegate.

NOW THAT WE HAVE ServiceUtils TO HELP WITH THE PLUMBING, WE MAKE A TwitterDelegate WHOSE JOB IT IS TO USE IT TO TALK TO TWITTER.

Creating the TwitterDelegate

In this section, we'll create the TwitterDelegate business delegate that will use the ServiceUtils class we've just seen. This class will be used in the commands (which we'll create next).

ch07/src/com/socialstalkr/business/TwitterDelegate.as

```
package com.socialstalkr.business {
  import com.socialstalkr.model.SocialStalkrModelLocator;
  import com.socialstalkr.util.ServiceUtils;
  import flash.net.URLRequest;
  import flash.net.navigateToURL;
  import mx.rpc.IResponder;

  public class TwitterDelegate {
    [Bindable]                                                    ❶
    private var _model:SocialStalkrModelLocator =
      SocialStalkrModelLocator.instance;
                                                                  ❷
    private var _responder:IResponder;

    public function TwitterDelegate(responder:IResponder) {
      _responder = responder;
    }

    public function verifyCredentials(twitterName:String,
    twitterPassword:String):void {                               ❸
      var url:String =
        "http://" + twitterName + ":" + twitterPassword +
        "@twitter.com/account/verify_credentials.xml";
      ServiceUtils.send(url, _responder);
    }
                                                                  ❹
    public function showUserFriends(twitterName:String):void {
      ServiceUtils.send("http://twitter.com/statuses/friends/" +
        twitterName + ".xml", _responder);
    }
                                                                  ❺
    public function showUserTweets(twitterName:String):void {
      ServiceUtils.send(
        "http://twitter.com/statuses/user_timeline/" +
        twitterName + ".xml", _responder);
    }
                                                                  ❻
    public function postTweet(tweet:String):void {
      ServiceUtils.send(
        "http://" + _model.userName + ":" + _model.userPassword +
        "@twitter.com/statuses/update.xml",
```

```
          _responder, {status:tweet});
      }

      public static function endSession():void {
        ServiceUtils.send("http://twitter.com/account/end_session");
        try {
          navigateToURL(new URLRequest("http://ruboss.com"),
            "_top");
        } catch (e:Error) {
        }
      }
    }
  }
}
```

① We create a reference to the shared `SocialStalkrModelLocator`.

② The `_responder` variable stores a reference to the `IResponder`, which will be passed to the `ServiceUtils.send` method, and end up responding to the service call.

③ The `verifyCredentials` method logs into Twitter with a username and password combination. Note the http://name:password@ twitter.com/ URL syntax, which my Ruboss partner Scott Patten showed me.

④ The `showUserFriends` method shows the friends of a Twitter user.

⑤ The `showUserTweets` method shows all the recent tweets of a Twitter user.

⑥ The `postTweet` method uses the http://name:password@twitter.com/ URL syntax to POST a new tweet to Twitter.

⑦ The `endSession` logs out from Twitter and redirects you to a very self-serving URL.

The `TwitterDelegate` contains the functions that do the real work for talking to Twitter. These functions all use the very handy `ServiceUtils.send()` method, invoked with the appropriate URLs.

Having created the business delegate, we'll now create the commands—including the commands that use this business delegate.

Creating the commands

The first command that we'll create will be the ShowFriendTweets command, which shows the tweets of one of the Twitter users you're following.

ch07/src/com/socialstalkr/command/ShowFriendTweets.as

```
package com.socialstalkr.command {
  import com.adobe.cairngorm.commands.ICommand;
  import com.adobe.cairngorm.control.CairngormEvent;
  import com.socialstalkr.business.TwitterDelegate;
  import com.socialstalkr.model.SocialStalkrModelLocator;
  import mx.collections.XMLListCollection;
  import mx.rpc.IResponder;

  public class ShowFriendTweets implements ICommand, IResponder {    ❶
    public function ShowFriendTweets() {
    }

    public function execute(event:CairngormEvent):void {             ❷
      var delegate:TwitterDelegate = new TwitterDelegate(this);
      delegate.showUserTweets(event.data.screen_name);              ❸
    }

    public function result(event:Object):void {
      SocialStalkrModelLocator.instance.selectedFriendTweets =
        new XMLListCollection(XMLList(event.result.children()));
    }                                                                ❹

    public function fault(event:Object):void {
      trace("fault: " + event);
    }
  }
}
```

Here we're creating a ShowFriendTweets command that implements ICommand and IResponder ❶. Its execute method creates a new TwitterDelegate ❷, which calls its showUserTweets ❸ method. When this returns, an XMLListCollection is constructed and assigned to the selectedFriendTweets in the shared SocialStalkrModelLocator ❹.

(At this point, you may begin to see how Cairngorm fits together.)

Next, we create a similar command, ShowUserFriends, to list a user's friends.

ch07/src/com/socialstalkr/command/ShowUserFriends.as

```
package com.socialstalkr.command {
  import com.adobe.cairngorm.commands.ICommand;
  import com.adobe.cairngorm.control.CairngormEvent;
  import com.socialstalkr.business.TwitterDelegate;
  import com.socialstalkr.model.SocialStalkrModelLocator;
  import mx.collections.XMLListCollection;
  import mx.rpc.IResponder;

  public class ShowUserFriends implements ICommand, IResponder {
    public function ShowUserFriends() {
    }

    public function execute(event:CairngormEvent):void {
      var delegate:TwitterDelegate = new TwitterDelegate(this);
      delegate.showUserFriends(event.data);             ①
    }

    public function result(event:Object):void {         ②
      SocialStalkrModelLocator.instance.twitterUserFriends =
        new XMLListCollection(XMLList(event.result.children()));
    }

    public function fault(event:Object):void {
      trace("fault: " + event);
    }
  }
}
```

This is very similar to what we just did in ShowFriendTweets. We create a ShowUserFriends command, which creates a new TwitterDelegate and calls its showUserFriends ① method. The ShowUserFriends command then constructs an XMLListCollection out of the result and assigns it ② to the shared SocialStalkrModelLocator twitterUserFriends.

If you think that was easy, it gets even easier to show the tweets of the selected user.

ch07/src/com/socialstalkr/command/ShowUserTweets.as

```
package com.socialstalkr.command {
  import com.adobe.cairngorm.commands.ICommand;
  import com.adobe.cairngorm.control.CairngormEvent;
  import com.socialstalkr.business.TwitterDelegate;
  import com.socialstalkr.control.EventNames;
  import com.socialstalkr.model.SocialStalkrModelLocator;
  import com.socialstalkr.util.CairngormUtils;
  import mx.collections.XMLListCollection;
  import mx.rpc.IResponder;

  public class ShowUserTweets implements ICommand, IResponder {
    [Bindable]
    private var _model:SocialStalkrModelLocator =
      SocialStalkrModelLocator.instance;

    public function ShowUserTweets() {
    }

    public function execute(event:CairngormEvent):void {
      var delegate:TwitterDelegate = new TwitterDelegate(this);
      delegate.showUserTweets(_model.userName);                ◁──── ❶
    }

    public function result(event:Object):void {
      var tweetsXLC:XMLListCollection =
        new XMLListCollection(XMLList(event.result.children()));
      _model.twitterUserTweets = tweetsXLC;                    ◁──── ❷
      if (tweetsXLC.length > 0) {
        var selectedTweet:XML = XML(tweetsXLC.getItemAt(0));
        if (_model.twitterUser == null) {
          _model.twitterUser = XML(selectedTweet.user);        ◁──── ❸
        } else {
          _model.selectedTweet = selectedTweet;
        }
      }
    }

    public function fault(event:Object):void {
      trace("fault: " + event);
    }
  }
}
```

We call showUserTweets ❶ again and just assign the result to a different variable in the SocialStalkrModelLocator: the twitterUserTweets ❷. We also check if we have any tweets, and if so, we set the XML of the current twitterUser ❸ based on the first tweet. Yes, this is cheesy, but it's necessary since there's currently no Twitter API call to get this directly. (Worse, if a user has no tweets, this code will break.)

Next, we create a VerifyCredentials command, which logs into Twitter. Again, this uses the TwitterDelegate.

ch07/src/com/socialstalkr/command/VerifyCredentials.as

```
package com.socialstalkr.command {
  import com.adobe.cairngorm.commands.ICommand;
  import com.adobe.cairngorm.control.CairngormEvent;
  import com.socialstalkr.business.TwitterDelegate;
  import com.socialstalkr.control.EventNames;
  import com.socialstalkr.model.SocialStalkrModelLocator;
  import com.socialstalkr.util.CairngormUtils;
  import mx.core.FlexGlobals;
  import mx.rpc.IResponder;

  public class VerifyCredentials implements ICommand, IResponder {
    [Bindable]
    private var _model:SocialStalkrModelLocator =
      SocialStalkrModelLocator.instance;

    public function VerifyCredentials() {
    }

    public function execute(event:CairngormEvent):void {     ❶
      _model.userName = event.data.twitterName;
      _model.userPassword = event.data.twitterPassword;
      var delegate:TwitterDelegate = new TwitterDelegate(this);
      delegate.verifyCredentials(_model.userName,
        _model.userPassword);                                ❷
    }

    public function result(event:Object):void {             ❸
      CairngormUtils.dispatchEvent(EventNames.SHOW_USER_TWEETS);
      CairngormUtils.dispatchEvent(EventNames.SHOW_USER_FRIENDS,
        _model.userName);
```

```
        FlexGlobals.topLevelApplication.currentState = "main";
    }

    public function fault(event:Object):void {
    }
  }
}
```

① We store the `twitterName` and `twitterPassword` in the `userName` and `userPassword` variables in the `_model`, for use when posting tweets.

② We then call the `verifyCredentials` method.

③ When the service call returns, we dispatch events that trigger the `ShowUserTweets` and `ShowUserFriends` commands.

Note how the result handler (which is called on successful return) triggers the execution of two other commands: `ShowUserTweets` and `ShowUserFriends` **③**. Recall that this association was defined with the `addCommand` calls in the `SocialStalkrController`.

Next up is the `PostTweet` command, which posts a new tweet to Twitter.

ch07/src/com/socialstalkr/command/PostTweet.as

```
package com.socialstalkr.command {
  import com.adobe.cairngorm.commands.ICommand;
  import com.adobe.cairngorm.control.CairngormEvent;
  import com.socialstalkr.business.TwitterDelegate;
  import com.socialstalkr.control.EventNames;
  import com.socialstalkr.util.CairngormUtils;
  import mx.rpc.IResponder;

  public class PostTweet implements ICommand, IResponder {
    public function PostTweet() {
    }

    public function execute(event:CairngormEvent):void {    ❶
      var delegate:TwitterDelegate = new TwitterDelegate(this);   ←┘
      delegate.postTweet(event.data);
    }

    public function result(event:Object):void {    ❷
      CairngormUtils.dispatchEvent(EventNames.SHOW_USER_TWEETS);   ←┘
```

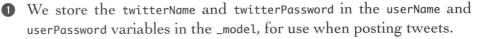

```
    }

    public function fault(event:Object):void {
    }
  }
}
```

1 We create a new `TwitterDelegate` with this command as the responder.

2 Once the new tweet is posted, we list the user tweets again.

When the `postTweet` **1** call returns, we just dispatch an event **2** to trigger the `ShowUserTweets` command. This is a simple way of ensuring our list is accurate (and that it includes tweets made from other Twitter clients). It's inefficient, though, and it will increase the speed that we use up our number of tweets per hour API limit. If we were building a real Twitter client we wouldn't do this.

Creating the visual components

Now that we've created so much of the plumbing, we turn to creating the visual components that use it. First, the `LoginPanel`— recall that it's shown in the `login` state of the main `SocialStalkr` application.

AT THE NEXT LEVEL UP THE FOOD CHAIN ARE THE VISUAL COMPONENTS. IT'S LIKE A KID'S BOOK: THE VISUAL COMPONENTS USE THE COMMANDS WHICH USE THE TwitterDelegate WHICH USES THE ServiceUtils (AT THE BOTTOM OF THE SEA). SO THE VISUAL COMPONENTS ARE AT THE TOP OF THE FOOD CHAIN.

ch07/src/com/socialstalkr/components/LoginPanel.mxml

```
<?xml version="1.0" encoding="utf-8"?>
<s:Panel xmlns:fx="http://ns.adobe.com/mxml/2009"
  xmlns:s="library://ns.adobe.com/flex/spark"
  xmlns:mx="library://ns.adobe.com/flex/halo"
  width="300" title="SocialStalkr - Login">
<fx:Script><![CDATA[
  import com.socialstalkr.util.CairngormUtils;
  import com.socialstalkr.control.EventNames;

  private function loadTwitterUser():void {
    CairngormUtils.dispatchEvent(EventNames.VERIFY_CREDENTIALS,    <── 1
    { twitterName: twitterNameTextInput.text,
      twitterPassword: twitterPasswordTextInput.text});
  }
```

```
]]></fx:Script>
<s:layout>
    <s:VerticalLayout paddingLeft="10" paddingTop="10"
        paddingRight="10" paddingBottom="10"/>
</s:layout>
  <s:Label text="Twitter Name" fontWeight="bold"/>
  <s:TextInput id="twitterNameTextInput" width="100%"
    text="peterarmstrong"/>
  <s:Label id="passwordLabel" text="Password"
    fontWeight="bold"/>
  <s:TextInput id="twitterPasswordTextInput" width="100%"
    displayAsPassword="true" enter="loadTwitterUser();"/>
  <s:Button id="loginButton" label="Login"
    click="loadTwitterUser();"/>
</s:Panel>
```

❶ Trigger the `VerifyCredentials` command, and pass the name and password along in an anonymous object.

❷ Use a vertical layout, which includes padding to make the controls look nicely spaced inside the `Panel`.

❸ Trigger the `loadTwitterUser` function on the Enter key being pressed in the `twitterPasswordTextInput` or the `loginButton` being clicked.

VISUAL COMPONENTS
AT THE TOP OF THE
FOOD CHAIN? HA!
I AM AT THE TOP OF
THE FOOD CHAIN.
I CAN REDESIGN
THINGS FOR RANDOM
"CREATIVE REASONS"
AND KEEP YOU CODERS
BUSY FOR DAYS WHILE
I HAVE A LIFE!

Now, with the past few pages demonstrating the verbosity of Cairngorm, we can start to see its benefits. Simply put, the business logic of logging in is nicely encapsulated from the UI controls that trigger it.

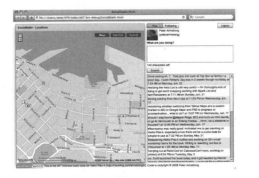

Next, after the login succeeds, the `SocialStalkr` app switches to the main state and shows the `MainApp`. Before we continue, I'm going to show the `MainApp` again, since this is what we're creating in the rest of the chapter.

Let's look at the code for the MainApp now.

ch07/src/com/socialstalkr/components/MainApp.mxml

```
<?xml version="1.0" encoding="utf-8"?>
<s:VGroup xmlns:fx="http://ns.adobe.com/mxml/2009"
  xmlns:s="library://ns.adobe.com/flex/spark"
  xmlns:mx="library://ns.adobe.com/flex/halo"
  xmlns:components="com.socialstalkr.components.*">
  <s:HGroup width="100%" height="100%" gap="10">          ❶
    <components:MapPanel/>
    <components:TwitterGroup/>
  </s:HGroup>
  <s:HGroup id="footerBox" width="100%" verticalAlign="middle">  ❷
    <s:BitmapImage source="@Embed('assets/websrv_120_1.gif')"/>
    <s:Label text="This is the MIT-licensed book code
for Hello! Flex 4 (http://manning.com/armstrong3/). Code is
copyright &#169; 2009 Peter Armstrong."/>                ❸
  </s:HGroup>
</s:VGroup>
```

❶ The MapPanel and TwitterGroup components are in an HGroup, which lays them out horizontally.

❷ The BitmapImage only supports embedded images (unlike an mx:Image, which can load URLs), so we embed Yahoo!'s image.

❸ We show the copyright notice in a Label. Note how the text attribute can span multiple lines without creating any extra spaces or newlines in the resulting string.

There's not much to the MainApp—it's just layout, really.

Next, we look at the components contained in the MainApp. First we have the MapPanel.

ch07/src/com/socialstalkr/components/MapPanel.mxml

```
<?xml version="1.0" encoding="utf-8"?>
<s:Panel xmlns:fx="http://ns.adobe.com/mxml/2009"
  xmlns:s="library://ns.adobe.com/flex/spark"
  xmlns:mx="library://ns.adobe.com/flex/halo"
  title="SocialStalkr - Locations" width="100%" height="100%"
  creationComplete="onCreationComplete()">
```

```
<fx:Script><![CDATA[
  import mx.binding.utils.BindingUtils;
  import mx.binding.utils.ChangeWatcher;
  import mx.events.ResizeEvent;
  import com.yahoo.maps.api.MapTypes;
  import com.yahoo.maps.api.YahooMapEvent;
  import com.yahoo.maps.api.YahooMap;
  import com.yahoo.maps.api.markers.Marker;
  import com.yahoo.maps.api.core.location.Address;
  import com.yahoo.maps.api.core.location.LatLon;
  import com.yahoo.maps.webservices.geocoder.GeocoderResult;
  import com.yahoo.maps.webservices.geocoder.events.GeocoderEvent;
  import com.socialstalkr.model.SocialStalkrModelLocator;
  import com.socialstalkr.components.TwitterMarker;                    ❶

  private static const YAHOO_APP_ID:String =
"TWLRFYTV34GhMOfRCZubCe_LcKgnCKtK06BYJy3WNYSg0d.MaEk1483y4_OpzxjlJEk-";

  [Bindable]
  private var _map:YahooMap;                                    ❷

  [Bindable]
  private var _model:SocialStalkrModelLocator =
    SocialStalkrModelLocator.instance;
                                                                   ❸
  private function onCreationComplete():void {
    BindingUtils.bindSetter(locateTweet, _model, "selectedTweet");
    _map = new YahooMap();                                    ❹
    _map.addEventListener(
      YahooMapEvent.MAP_INITIALIZE, onMapInitialize);
    _map.init(YAHOO_APP_ID, mapContainer.width,
      mapContainer.height);
    _map.addPanControl();
    _map.addScaleBar();
    _map.addTypeWidget();
    _map.addZoomWidget();
    mapContainer.addEventListener(ResizeEvent.RESIZE,
      onMapResize);
    mapContainer.addChild(_map);
  }
...
```

❶ Be sure to use your own Yahoo! App ID, not this. (That's why it's in ~~strikethrough~~.)

② This is the YahooMap we're displaying.

③ BindingUtils.bindSetter listens to the data binding events to trigger the locateTweet function call. This saves us from having to try to call locateTweet from a Cairngorm command, which is brittle.

④ We initialize the YahooMap. Note how we create the component, initialize it, attach listeners, and then add it to the containment hierarchy—this ensures it (and its parents) are ready for the events that will get fired.

So far, we have added a const (meaning it doesn't change) for our YAHOO_APP_ID **①**. Do *not* use this one: use the one you got when you signed up with Yahoo!. Next, we add a variable called _map for the YahooMap **②**, and in the onCreationComplete event handler function we set a bunch of fairly self-explanatory properties, including initializing the _map **④**. Let's look at the rest of the code in this file now.

ch07/src/com/socialstalkr/components/MapPanel.mxml (continued)

```
...
  private function locateTweet(tweet:XML):void {                    ⟵———⑤
    if (tweet == null) return;
    //_map.markerManager.removeAllMarkers();//broke in Flex 4 Beta 2;
    var text:String = tweet.text;
    var points:Array = text.match(/@{(.*)}/);
    var profileImageUrl:String = tweet.user.profile_image_url;
    var name:String = tweet.user.name;
    var location:String = tweet.user.location;

    if (points != null && points.length > 0) {
      var address:Address = new Address(points[1]);
      var marker:Marker = new TwitterMarker(
        profileImageUrl, text.replace(points[0], points[1]));
      marker.address = address;
      _map.markerManager.addMarker(marker);
      geocodeAddress(address);
    }
  }
                                                                        ⑥
  private function onMapResize(event:ResizeEvent):void {            ⟵┐
    _map.setSize(mapContainer.width, mapContainer.height);
  }
```

```
  private function onMapInitialize(event:YahooMapEvent):void {
    _map.zoomLevel = 3;
    var address:Address =
      new Address("21 Water Street, Vancouver, BC");
    geocodeAddress(address);
  }

  private function geocodeAddress(address:Address):void {
    address.addEventListener(
      GeocoderEvent.GEOCODER_SUCCESS, onGeocoderSuccess);
    address.geocode();
  }

  private function onGeocoderSuccess(event:GeocoderEvent):void {
    var result:GeocoderResult =
      event.data.firstResult as GeocoderResult;
    _map.centerLatLon = result.latlon;
  }
]]></fx:Script>
  <mx:UIComponent id="mapContainer" width="100%" height="100%"/>
</s:Panel>
```

7 **8** **9** **10**

Let's take a tour of the rest of this code.

We start by creating a function called locateTweet **5**, which gets called whenever the _model.selectedTweet changes because of the use of the BindingUtils.bindSetter function **3**. (BindingUtils let you set up binding expressions in ActionScript code.) Note that the removeAllMarkers() library function call got broken by Flex 4 Beta 2. It may be working by the time you read this, so I'm leaving this line in but commented out. (The app will work either way.)

The approach in locateTweet is a bit subtle: it checks to see if the text of the tweet contains text that matches the regular expression /@{(.*)}/, which means that text like "I'm at @{21 Water St, Vancouver} writing the book" will match but text like "I'm at 21 Water Street, Vancouver writing the book" will not. Specifically, the text "I'm at @{21 Water St, Vancouver} writing the book" will produce a points Array whose 0th element is "@{21 Water St, Vancouver}" and whose 1st element is "21 Water St, Vancouver". So, we then check if we have a non-null points Array with a length of greater than 0, meaning if we have a match. If we do have a match, we create a new TwitterMarker with the profileImageUrl and with the text. Note that we replace the points Array's 0th element, such as "@{21 Water St, Vancouver}", with the points Array's 1st element, such as "21 Water St, Vancouver", in order to make the marker text look nicer. We also set the address with the points Array's 1st element and then set the address of the marker to the address. We then add the marker to the _map's markerManager, and then call our geocodeAddress function ❽, which geocodes the address and centers the map on that latitude and longitude on a successful result ❾.

Next, we add a function called onMapResize ❻, which ensures the map is correctly sized when the map is resized (say, if its parent UIComponent ❿ grows if the application grows if the user makes the browser window larger).

We then add an onMapInitialize ❼ function, which sets the map to an arbitrary, fairly zoomed in zoom level of 3, an appropriate zoom level for "stalking" our friends who are embedding their special location tags in their tweets. We also start with an arbitrary Address. I'd have liked to have used your IP address as a basis for geocoding, but I don't think this is possible to be done in pure client-side Flex code.

Having created the map, we turn to the task of creating a marker class that shows the user's avatar and tweet. We'll use this class for tweets that have location tags and that can be shown on the map. (Thanks to Dima Berastau for this code and help with the explanation!)

ch07/src/com/socialstalkr/components/TwitterMarker.as

```
package com.socialstalkr.components {
  import com.yahoo.maps.api.markers.Marker;

  import flash.display.Loader;
  import flash.display.Shape;
  import flash.events.Event;
  import flash.net.URLRequest;
  import flash.system.LoaderContext;
  import flash.text.TextField;
  import flash.text.TextFormat;

  public class TwitterMarker extends Marker {        ❶
    private var _shape:Shape;
    private var _loader:Loader;
```

```
    private var _url:String;
    private var _textField:TextField;
    private var _text:String;
                                                                    ❷
    public function TwitterMarker(url:String, text:String) {   ←⎯
      super();
      _url = url;
      _text = text;                            ❸
      _shape = new Shape();                ←⎯
      _shape.graphics.lineStyle(1,0x666666);
      _shape.graphics.beginFill(0xFFFFFF,1);
      _shape.graphics.drawRoundRect(5, 5, 250, 51, 0, 0);
      _shape.graphics.endFill();                       ❹
      addChild(_shape);
      _loader = new Loader();                      ←⎯
      _loader.contentLoaderInfo.addEventListener(Event.COMPLETE,
        onLoadComplete);
      _loader.load(new URLRequest(url), new LoaderContext(true));
      addChild(_loader);
      _textField = new TextField();                 ←⎯
      _textField.text = text;
      _textField.cacheAsBitmap = true;              ❺
      _textField.defaultTextFormat =
        new TextFormat("Arial", 11, 0x000000, true);
      _textField.wordWrap = true;
      _textField.x = 57;
      _textField.y = 7;
      _textField.width = 200;
      _textField.height = 65;
      addChild(_textField);
    }

    private function onLoadComplete(event:Event):void {
      _loader.x = 7;
      _loader.y = 7;
      _loader.height = 48;
      _loader.width = 48;
    }
  }
}
```

We are creating a component called TwitterMarker, which extends the
Marker ❶ class provided by Yahoo!. The Marker is not a Flex component like TextInput, List, or VBox—instead, it's a direct subclass of

flash.display.Sprite (more about this in the accompanying sidebar). In this class's constructor ❷, we store the URL of an image to display, as well as the text to display.

This class shows that if you want to, you can use lower-level components from the flash packages.

To achieve our objective and display a friend's tweet as a marker on our Yahoo! map, we'll have to create a few native Flash objects and use their programmatic graphics API directly. In our case we'll start by creating a Shape ❸, define its lineStyle to be 1 pixel wide, and make it use a nice gray (0x666666). (The Shape class creates lightweight shapes using the AS3 drawing API, and includes a graphics property so you can call Graphics methods. A Shape is lighter weight than a Sprite, since it can't contain display objects or handle mouse events.)

Next we'll specify that our shape should have a white background. Note that we still haven't indicated what *shape* we actually want. Should it be a circle, a line, or something else? We call the drawRoundRect() method to use a rounded rectangle with a height of 51 pixels and a width of 250 pixels. Finally, we call the endFill() method to finish the creation of the shape. Now that our shape is ready, we need to add it as a child to the TwitterMarker object (using the addChild(_shape) method, which is equivalent to calling this.addChild(_shape)). All we're accomplishing with this is adding our newly created shape to the Flash object graph. Until we added the shape *somewhere*, Flash wouldn't know what all this drawing should happen relative to. (We add this Shape instance to draw a background shape for our marker, since Marker by default has no shape.)

Now that we have a rounded box drawn on the map at the exact location we specified when creating the TwitterMarker instance, let's tackle our next challenge, which is loading the user image specified as a url argument in the TwitterMarker constructor. Since this is going to be an asynchronous operation, we have to use Flash Loader ❹ object, which will go out and fetch the image bytes from the URL we specified and load them into the Flash runtime. Again, we add the Loader as a child of the TwitterMarker instance. Last but not least, we'll create a Flash TextField ❺ to display the actual tweet. TextField is a low-level object that's used to render text. We set its properties, such as the font type, and add it as a child to the current `TwitterMarker` instance.

Anyway, that said, all this class does is draw the text and image for the marker with the avatar and tweet; we don't need to get bogged down in the advanced details about mixing and matching Flash and Flex components.

No fair! I'm an experienced developer! I want the advanced details!

OK, fine. Here's what Dima Berastau has to say about this:

When you first encounter Flex, your primary activities will mostly revolve around developing MXML components and self-contained AS3 objects. Seasoned Java developers might think, "Awesome! This is easy. AS3 is almost like Java and MXML is just a domain-specific language for laying out the UI declaratively. Nothing new here." The Flash platform will be simply a runtime that your compiled code runs on. After all, you don't go around messing with JVM byte code in Java.

Not true. Fortunately or unfortunately, the Flash platform is not just a runtime detail. In some advanced situations, you'll be in a position where you'll need to write code that uses Flash constructs directly, bypassing all the Flex component machinery. Integrating with third-party components such as Yahoo! Maps is a great example of this: we want to display your friends' tweets as markers on a Yahoo! map embedded in your Flex application. However, the `YahooMap` and the `Marker` classes aren't Flex components—they just both directly subclass `flash.display.Sprite`.

Although you might be tempted to try to add a new marker to the map by doing something like calling `addChild(new TextInput())`, this won't have the desired effect of displaying a `TextInput` element over some location on the map. Flex components have a much more complex lifecycle compared to basic Flash objects and, as such, don't play well together.

Next, we create the `TwitterGroup` class, which displays the content to the right of the map.

ch07/src/com/socialstalkr/components/TwitterGroup.mxml

```
<?xml version="1.0" encoding="utf-8"?>
<s:VGroup xmlns:fx="http://ns.adobe.com/mxml/2009"
  xmlns:s="library://ns.adobe.com/flex/spark"
  xmlns:mx="library://ns.adobe.com/flex/halo"
  xmlns:components="com.socialstalkr.components.*"
  width="380" height="100%">
```

```
<fx:Script><![CDATA[
  import mx.collections.ArrayCollection;
  import spark.events.IndexChangeEvent;
  import com.socialstalkr.business.TwitterDelegate;

  [Bindable]                                                              ❶
  private var _buttonData:ArrayCollection = new ArrayCollection([
    {label: "You", data: "you"},
    {label: "Following", data: "following"}]);

  private function changeSelection(event:IndexChangeEvent): void {
    currentState = _buttonData[event.newIndex].data;                     ❷
  }
]]></fx:Script>
  <s:states>
    <s:State name="you"/>                                               ❸
    <s:State name="following"/>
  </s:states>
  <s:Group width="100%">
    <s:ButtonBar id="viewMenu" selectedIndex="0"
      change="changeSelection(event)" labelField="label"
      dataProvider="{_buttonData}" left="0"/>                           ❹
    <s:Button label="Logout" click="TwitterDelegate.endSession();"
      right="0"/>                                                        ❺
  </s:Group>
  <components:YouGroup includeIn="you"/>
  <components:FollowingGroup includeIn="following"/>                     ❻
</s:VGroup>
```

❶ The `_buttonData ArrayCollection` is used as the `dataProvider` of the `ButtonBar`.

❷ The `changeSelection` function sets the state of the component to the data property of the object in the `_buttonData` `Array` at the `event.newIndex`, which will be either you or `following`.

❸ These are the states that the `TwitterGroup` can be in. This use of view states, along with the use of the `ButtonBar`, is essentially what a `TabNavigator` would've been used for in Flex 3.

❹ The `ButtonBar` specifies a `labelField` of `label`, meaning that the buttons will show either You or Following, which are the `label` properties of the anonymous objects in the `_buttonData ArrayCollection`.

❺ Create a `Logout` button that just calls the `endSession` function directly, as we didn't bother to create a command for logout.

6 The `YouGroup` and `FollowingGroup` components are in only one view state each.

Note that I did not use a `TabNavigator` since it can only contain Halo children, and I'm trying to use Spark components wherever possible in this app.

Next up, we create the `YouGroup` and `FollowingGroup` components contained in the `TwitterGroup` component.

ch07/src/com/socialstalkr/components/YouGroup.mxml

```xml
<?xml version="1.0" encoding="utf-8"?>
<s:Group xmlns:fx="http://ns.adobe.com/mxml/2009"
  xmlns:s="library://ns.adobe.com/flex/spark"
  xmlns:mx="library://ns.adobe.com/flex/halo"
  width="100%" height="100%">
<fx:Script><![CDATA[
  import com.socialstalkr.business.TwitterDelegate;
  import com.socialstalkr.control.EventNames;
  import com.socialstalkr.model.SocialStalkrModelLocator;
  import com.socialstalkr.util.CairngormUtils;

  [Bindable]
  private var _model:SocialStalkrModelLocator =
    SocialStalkrModelLocator.instance;

  private function locateTweet(tweet:XML):void {
    _model.selectedTweet = tweet;
  }

  private function postTweet(tweet:String):void {
    CairngormUtils.dispatchEvent(EventNames.POST_TWEET, tweet);     <--- 1
  }
]]></fx:Script>
  <s:layout>
    <s:VerticalLayout/>
  </s:layout>
  <s:HGroup width="100%">
    <mx:Image width="48" height="48"                                 2
      source="{_model.twitterUser.profile_image_url}"/>            <---
    <s:VGroup width="100%">
```

```
      <s:Label width="100%"
        text="{_model.twitterUser.name}"/>
      <s:Label width="100%"
        text="({_model.twitterUser.screen_name})"/>      ③
    </s:VGroup>
  </s:HGroup>
  <s:VGroup width="100%">
    <s:Label text="What are you doing?" fontWeight="bold"/>
    <s:TextArea id="postTA" width="100%" height="75"/>       ④
    <s:Label text="{140 - postTA.text.length} characters left"
      color="{(postTA.text.length > 140) ? 0xFF0000 : 0x000000}"/>
    <s:Button enabled="{postTA.text.length &lt;= 140}"
      label="Submit" click="postTweet(postTA.text)"/>
  </s:VGroup>
  <mx:List id="selectedUserTweetList"                   ⑤
    width="100%" height="100%" labelFunction="{_model.formatTweet}"
    paddingTop="0" paddingBottom="0" paddingLeft="0" paddingRight="0"
    change="locateTweet(XML(selectedUserTweetList.selectedItem))"
    dataProvider="{_model.twitterUserTweets}"
    alternatingItemColors="[#EEEEEE, #FFFFFF]"
    wordWrap="true" variableRowHeight="true" borderStyle="none"/>
</s:Group>
```

❶ Posting a tweet just triggers the PostTweet command. People like to pick on it, but hooray for Cairngorm!

❷ The Halo Image class is used here because the Spark BitmapImage class can't handle nonembedded images.

❸ We bind to the _model for various shared properties, like the name.

❹ Data binding also works nicely to calculate things like the number of characters left in a tweet. Note how XML's restrictions against < and > inside attribute values forces the use of <= for <=.

❺ We use the Halo List class since the Spark List class is terrible at word wrapping.

As this example shows, Flex 4 apps can still use help from the old Halo components. It also shows how the shared state in the Model Locator pattern is used by Cairngorm. Depending on your taste and on the size of apps you typically build, this is either nice and simple or else a distasteful, thinly disguised use of global state.

Next up, we create a FollowingGroup class for the Twitter users we're following. Recall that this app shows a List of them at the top and the tweets of the selected friend at the bottom.

ch07/src/com/socialstalkr/components/FollowingGroup.mxml

```xml
<?xml version="1.0" encoding="utf-8"?>
<s:Group xmlns:fx="http://ns.adobe.com/mxml/2009"
  xmlns:s="library://ns.adobe.com/flex/spark"
  xmlns:mx="library://ns.adobe.com/flex/halo"
  width="100%" height="100%">
<fx:Script><![CDATA[
  import spark.events.IndexChangeEvent;
  import com.socialstalkr.business.TwitterDelegate;
  import com.socialstalkr.control.EventNames;
  import com.socialstalkr.model.SocialStalkrModelLocator;
  import com.socialstalkr.util.CairngormUtils;

  [Bindable]                                                        ❶
  private var _model:SocialStalkrModelLocator =
    SocialStalkrModelLocator.instance;

  private function onUserSelect(event:IndexChangeEvent):void {      ❷
    _model.selectedFriend =
      XML(spark.components.List(event.currentTarget).selectedItem);
    CairngormUtils.dispatchEvent(EventNames.SHOW_FRIEND_TWEETS,
      _model.selectedFriend);
  }
                                                                   ❸
  private function locateTweet(tweet:XML):void {
    _model.selectedTweet = tweet;
  }
]]></fx:Script>
<s:layout>
      <s:VerticalLayout/>
</s:layout>
  <s:Panel width="100%" height="250"
    title="{_model.twitterUser.name} is Following">
    <s:List id="usersList" width="100%" height="100%"              ❹
      dataProvider="{_model.twitterUserFriends}"
      change="onUserSelect(event)"
itemRenderer="com.socialstalkr.components.UserListItemRenderer"/>
  </s:Panel>
```

```
    <s:Panel visible="{_model.selectedFriend != null}"
      width="100%" height="100%"
      title="{_model.selectedFriend.name}'s Tweets">
      <mx:List id="selectedFriendTweetList"
        width="100%" height="100%" borderStyle="none"
        alternatingItemColors="[#EEEEEE, #FFFFFF]"
        paddingTop="0" paddingBottom="0" paddingLeft="0"
        paddingRight="0" wordWrap="true" variableRowHeight="true"
        change="locateTweet(XML(selectedFriendTweetList.selectedItem))"
        labelFunction="{_model.formatTweet}"
        dataProvider="{_model.selectedFriendTweets}"/>
    </s:Panel>
  </s:Group>
```

⑤

❶ Get a reference to the SocialStalkrModelLocator singleton.

❷ When a user is selected, we assign the shared `selectedFriend` variable and show that friend's tweets. Note how I'm using the fully qualified class name of the Spark `List` (`spark.components.List`) since both Halo and Spark `List` classes are used here.

❸ The `locateTweet` function just sets the shared `selectedTweet` variable, which triggers the binding in the `MapPanel`.

❹ We use a Spark `List` here with a custom `itemRenderer`.

❺ We use a Halo `List` here since we need word wrapping.

Again, here we're being negligent about caching, and we're just showing the friend's tweets every time we select them. This repeated use will often hit the Twitter rate cap, so don't do this if you're building a real Twitter client!

One more component left! Finally, we need to build the custom `Item-Renderer` for the Spark `List` of the Twitter users we're following.

ch07/src/com/socialstalkr/components/UserListItemRenderer.mxml

```
<?xml version="1.0" encoding="utf-8"?>
<s:ItemRenderer xmlns:fx="http://ns.adobe.com/mxml/2009"
  xmlns:s="library://ns.adobe.com/flex/spark"
  xmlns:mx="library://ns.adobe.com/flex/halo">
<fx:Script><![CDATA[
  [Bindable]
  private var _value:XML;
```

```
  [Bindable]
  public override function set data(value:Object):void {          ⟵
    _value = XML(value);                                                    ❶
  }

  public override function get data():Object {
    return _value;
  }
]]></fx:Script>
  <s:states>                                                      ❷
    <s:State name="normal"/>                                      ⟵
    <s:State name="hovered" stateGroups="big"/>
    <s:State name="selected" stateGroups="big"/>
  </s:states>
  <s:HGroup width="100%" color.selected="0x990066"
    color.hovered="0x0000FF">                                     ❸
    <mx:Image id="profileImage" width="20" height="20"            ⟵
      width.big="48" height.big="48"
      source="{_value.profile_image_url}"/>
    <s:VGroup id="summaryArea">
      <s:Label text="{_value.name}"/>
      <s:Label fontStyle="italic" includeIn="big"                 ⟵
        text="({_value.screen_name})"/>                           ❹
    </s:VGroup>
  </s:HGroup>
</s:ItemRenderer>
```

❶ We override the data setter and getter, and store the _value as XML. The component that's using this as its itemRenderer sets the data property, which is what this set function in the ItemRenderer subclass takes advantage of.

❷ We create the required states for a Spark ItemRenderer. Note the use of the stateGroups attribute: we're creating a "big" StateGroup to refer to both the hovered and selected states. Note that the normal, hovered, and selected states are *required state names* for Spark ItemRenderers to have!

❸ We use a Halo Image here since its source isn't embedded.

❹ The includeIn attribute can take StateGroups as well as just States.

CAUTION Flex 3 programmers take note: if you don't define the required normal, hovered, and selected states for your Spark ItemRenderers, your app will explode!

That's it! Click Play to compile and run the application. Log in with your Twitter ID; you'll see the app shown in the beginning of the chapter. If you then post a tweet with a location coded like @{some address that Yahoo can parse}, you should be able to click on that tweet and see a nice marker displayed on the map, centered over your location. When you click on tweets with no @{location} tags, no marker is shown on the map.

Key points

- For an application of this size, Cairngorm is probably overkill. However, this is an introductory book, so we don't have the space to build an application that's large enough to demonstrate the benefits.

- Cairngorm is a useful way of structuring large Flex applications. With the switch to Flex 4, it will be interesting to see whether Mate, Swiz, or PureMVC can dethrone it.

- Despite its benefits, Cairngorm is verbose. You can tell that it owes its origin to a bunch of J2EE patterns—a fact that deserves some discussion. Flex is only possible because of the evolution of the Flash platform, and in many ways it's the future of the Flash platform. However, there's some tension here—some of the changes haven't been welcomed universally. Colin Moock wrote about this in his article "The Charges Against ActionScript 3.0," at www.insideria.com/2008/07/the-charges-against-actionscri.html. At a very high level, it's as though Flash has grown up from being a punk rock teenager to a mortgage broker—some of the people who knew it "back in the day" may wonder if it's forgetting its past. However, the roots are still there: Flex does compile to Flash, which means that much more is possible than traditional desktop or web UI developers are used to. Besides, Flex and Flash are being a lot more unified with Flex 4—*so much so that Flex Builder has been renamed to Flash Builder 4.* So Flash is Flex, and Flex is Flash, and they were all rebranded happily ever after.

- Flex is great at talking to web services, and HTTPService makes it easy to talk to RESTful services. (You can find out more about this in *Flexible Rails*, and also explore the RestfulX framework to see the ideas that began with *Flexible Rails* taken to the next level.)

What's next?

*THAT'S IT!
THANKS FOR
READING MY
BOOK! NOW GO
BUILD
SOMETHING COOL!*

That's it for this book. I really hope you enjoyed it, and that the cartoons gave you a couple of laughs as you learned the basics of Flex. Please email me at peter@ruboss.com with your feedback—good, bad, or both. If you'd like to share your comments with other readers, please post them to Manning's Author Online forum at www.manning.com/HelloFlex4.

Finally, I hope you build something cool using Flex 4. You're definitely way past the "Hello World" level as a Flex developer now...

Index